The Hungry God

David Shulman

The Hungry God

Hindu Tales of Filicide and Devotion

The University of Chicago Press
Chicago and London

David Shulman is a professor in the Department of Indian, Iranian, and Armenian Studies at the Hebrew University of Jerusalem.

The University of Chicago Press, Chicago 60637
The University of Chicago Press, Ltd., London

Printed in the United States of America
02 01 00 99 98 97 96 95 94 93   1 2 3 4 5
ISBN: 0-226-75571-1(cloth)

Library of Congress Cataloging-in-Publication Data

Shulma, David Dean, 1949–
The hungry god : Hindu tales of filicide and devotion / David Shulman.
p.   cm.
Includes bibliographical references and index.
1. Child sacrifice.   2. Sacrifice—Hinduism.   I. Title.
BL1236.76.S23S58   1993
294.5′34—dc20   93-18495
CIP

⊗The paper used in this publication meets the minimum requirements of the American National Standard for Information Sciences—Permanence of Paper for Printed Library Materials, ANSI Z39.48-1984.

For Sidra and Yaron
Shlomit and Richie—
yedidei nefesh

Contents

Acknowledgments

Jim Ponet suggested, or insisted, that I write this book, but in the end it wrote itself, with much welcome help from friends and students. Conceived as a set of short essays on the relations of metaphysics and emotion, the following chapters show what happens when one teaches Sanskrit in Jerusalem. It is difficult consistently to resist comparisons. In Israel the *aqedah* story is always close to the surface; simply to mention it often suffices to elicit a rich response. Among those who kindly, sometimes passionately shared with me their insights, I wish to thank in particular:

Meir Shahar, who wrote a penetrating paper on the Little Devotee in my seminar on Tamil Śaivism; Miri Sharf and Melila Helner-Eshed, for discussions of this story and its Biblical counterpart; Aviva Zornberg, for illuminating the Midrashic and later Jewish sources with subtlety and startling lucidity, and for allowing me to read her chapters on *Vayera* and *Chayei Sarah;* Wendy Doniger, A. K. Ramanujan, Paula Richman, Shmuel Erlich, Sidra Ezrahi, Henry Abramovitch, Don Handelman, Jerome Gellman, and Hananya Goodman, for long talks, patient listening, bibliographic aid, much helpful criticism of the first draft, and ever-dependable enthusiasm; Micky Shulman, for providing humane and loving space when I began to write things down.

Yigal and Galila Bronner journeyed to Lepakshi to photograph the Siriyāla panels for this book; for this, and for the privilege of teaching them, I am deeply grateful. Judy Jacobs at Hatzalmaniya skillfully developed these Lepakshi prints.

For miraculously creating space and freedom, on many levels, and making room to play, I wish to thank the John D. and Catherine T. MacArthur Foundation.

Velcheru Narayana Rao, with characteristic generosity and love, twice read with me Śrīnātha's Telugu version of the Siriyāla story and commented incisively on it. Chapter 3 should be seen as a joint effort reflecting our work together. No words could express the gratitude I feel for this teaching and companionship.

As always, the inner movement, behind the words, is for Eileen.

1
Introduction

Here are two stark and ancient stories, one from the Hebrew Bible, the other from Vedic India:

"And after these matters, God put Abraham to the test, and said to him: 'Abraham'—And he said, 'I am here.' And he said: 'Take your son, your only one, the one you love—Isaac—and go to the land of Moriah, and offer him there on one of the mountains that I will tell you.' So Abraham rose early in the morning and saddled his ass and took his two servant-boys with him, and his son Isaac; and he split logs for the offering, and rose and went to the place that God told him.

"On the third day, Abraham raised his eyes and saw the place from a distance. Abraham said to his boys, 'Remain here with the ass, while I and the boy go our way; we will bow down and return to you.' And Abraham took the logs for the offering and placed them on his son, Isaac; and he took in his hand the fire and the knife; and the two walked together.

"Then Isaac said to Abraham, his father: 'Father'—And he answered, 'I am here, my son.' And he said: 'Here are the fire and the logs, but where is the sheep to be sacrificed?' And Abraham said, 'God will see to the sheep for the sacrifice, my son.' And the two walked together.

"When they came to the place that God told him, Abraham

built an altar there and arranged the logs; and he bound his son Isaac, putting him on the altar, on top of the logs. Then Abraham reached for the knife, to slaughter his son. But a messenger of God called to him from the sky, 'Abraham, Abraham'—and he said, 'I am here.' And he said, 'Do not reach for the boy. Do nothing to him—for now I know that you are in awe of God, for you did not hold back your only son from me.'

"Abraham raised his eyes and saw a ram, behind him, caught in a thicket by its horns. So Abraham went and took the ram and sacrificed it in place of his son. And Abraham named that place 'God will see'; as even today it is said, 'on the mountain of God it is seen.'

"And God's messenger called to Abraham a second time from the sky: 'I swear by myself—so God says—that because you have done this thing and not held back your only son, I will bless you and multiply your seed like the stars of heaven and the sand on the shore of the sea; and your seed will inherit the gate of its enemies. All the peoples of the world will be blessed through your seed, since you listened to my voice.' And Abraham returned to his boys; they rose and went to Beersheba; and Abraham remained in Beersheba."[1]

"Bhṛgu, the son of Varuṇa, was devoted to learning. He thought that he was better than his father, better than the gods, better than the other Brahmins who were devoted to learning. Varuṇa thought to himself, 'My son does not know anything at all. Come, let us teach him to know something.' He took away his life's breaths, and Bhṛgu fainted[2] and went beyond this world.

"Bhṛgu arrived in the world beyond. There he saw a man cut another man to pieces and eat him. He said, 'Has this really happened? What is this?' They said to him, 'Ask Varuṇa, your father. He will tell you about this.' He came to a second world, where a man was eating another man, who was screaming. He said, 'Has this really happened? What is this?' They said to him, 'Ask Varuṇa, your father. He will tell you about this.' He went on to another world, where he saw a man eating another man, who was

1. Genesis 22 (my translation).
2. Or suffocated, choked to death (*tatāma*).

The binding of Isaac. Notice the ram, the angel's hand, and the two servants waiting with the ass. Early 6th-century mosaic, Bet Alpha Synagogue. Courtesy Palphot Ltd., Herzlia.

soundlessly screaming; then to another, where two women were guarding a great treasure; then to a fifth, where there were two streams on an even level, one filled with blood and one filled with butter. A naked black man with a club guarded the stream filled with blood; out of the stream filled with butter, men made of gold were drawing up all desires with bowls of gold. In the sixth world there were five rivers with blue lotuses and white lotuses, flowing with honey like water. In them there were dancing and singing, the sound of the lute, crowds of celestial nymphs [Apsarases], a fragrant smell, and a great sound.

"Bhṛgu returned from that world and came to Varuṇa, who said, 'Did you arrive, my son?' 'I arrived, father.' 'Did you see, my son?' 'I saw, father.' 'What, my son?' 'A man cut another man to pieces and ate him.' 'Yes,' said Varuṇa; 'when people in this world offer no oblation and lack true knowledge, but cut down trees and lay them on the fire, those trees take the form of men in the other world and eat [those people] in return.' 'How can one avoid that *(niṣkṛti)*?' 'When you put fuel on the sacred fire, that is how you avoid it and are free of it.' "

[In this way Varuṇa explained each of the images Bhṛgu had seen, and how to avoid them; and he identified the final worlds as his own—to be reached by the *agnihotra* offering. He who offers the *agnihotra* with true knowledge eludes the dangers witnessed by Bhṛgu in his journey.][3]

Do these stories resonate with one another in any way? In the first, God speaks, and a father is ready to sacrifice his son. A further voice from heaven—is it God's voice again, through another persona?—stops the sacrifice at the last second, before it can be completed. In the Vedic tale, the father seems impelled from within toward a similar act of slaughter; here the context is one of overt rivalry between father and son, and what is at stake is not only the child's life or death but, perhaps even more emphatically, the knowledge that this child does or does not possess. The son believes he has great learning, greater even than his father's; the father thinks the son knows nothing at all. An act of violence—strangling the son—puts these propositions to the test. Moreover, Varuṇa is himself a god, endowed with a transcendent wisdom which he ultimately demonstrates by interpreting each of the nightmare images his son has seen; in this sense, and in light of the overriding importance of such esoteric wisdom in the Vedic world, Bhṛgu's traumatic journey is no less the function of a divine imperative than is Isaac's ascent to Mount Moriah.

Both stories center on the theme of a father's violence, metaphysically motivated, toward his own son. In one case, this violent impulse is checked, the sacrifice aborted; in the other, nothing is possible unless the child actually dies. Yet in both texts an ambiguity remains on the level of mutuality and shared experience: two climb the mountain together (as the Biblical text tells us *twice*), but how many come down? "And Abraham returned to his boys"—the verb is singular. Did Isaac refuse to come home, after what he had seen? Was this offering truly averted, or subverted through substitution, as the text seems explicitly to assert? A long tradition of commentary begins here, with this singular verb and the doubt that it so elegantly and elliptically conceals.

3. *Jaiminīya Brāhmaṇa* 1.42–44, summarized by Doniger [O'Flaherty] (1985), 32–34; cf. *Śatapatha Brāhmaṇa* 11.6.1.1–13, and discussion by Doniger (1985), 35–49. ©1985 by The University of Chicago.

As to Bhṛgu, an unsettling, intensifying loneliness must accompany the visual trials that he undergoes—and note that this theme of testing is no less integral to the Vedic than to the Biblical text. Varuṇa puts his son through the travail of initiation, where this son must learn to see what his father already knows. It is not an easy path to maturity and self-knowledge. Alone, Bhṛgu is lost, uncertain, overpowered; he sees but cannot understand; terror and confusion pervade his travel through the other worlds. Only the father's absolute knowledge can extricate him from this haunted state—though it is his father who has forced the dreadful images on him in the first place. Moreover, a characteristic ontic quandary plagues the boy from the beginning; again and again, he asks, "Has this really happened?" *(abhūd batêdam)*—as if reluctant to credit the surrealistic visions that he must, on another level, internalize as his own. Truly to see, for the Vedic hero, is to confront men devouring other men; truly to know is to penetrate the meaning of these predatory images and inner truths. Isaac, on the other hand, sets off in trust, which is only slowly, belatedly, infiltrated by the terrible question, "Where is the sheep to be sacrificed?" From this point, after Abraham's pregnant response, silence envelops both figures; soon Isaac will see his father raise his arm, will see the glistening knife. The Midrash tells us, with characteristic boldness and psychological precision, that it was from that moment on that Isaac became blind.[4]

Bhṛgu sees, and fails to perceive; his terror translates into a bewildering uncertainty. Isaac looks up and goes blind. Abraham hears two voices, over three days, and decides that both are God's (but can he be sure? Do they well up from within him, or are they external? What does God's voice sound like?). The ambiguity of vision in the Vedic text is matched by the ambiguous hearing of the Biblical tale. And Bhṛgu, too, hears strange voices—the screams, some of them swallowed up in silence, of dying men. These sounds, too, are heavy with meaning, which the dead boy-wanderer cannot fathom. Moreover, both texts keep drifting off, themselves, into open-ended silences, broken by tantalizing, laconic speech. The intense inner experiences of the protagonists can only be inferred. Both texts seem entirely inhabited by males,

4. *Midrash Rabbah,* Bereshit 65:10.

powerful and dangerous fathers and rather passive sons; the mothers, whom we know to exist, are hidden away, somewhere out of sight.

And so on. We could easily go on comparing these two tales in this somewhat technical manner, amplifying both similarities and divergences in theme and tone. But let us rather rephrase our initial question. It is not, after all, simply a matter of resonances and/or suggestive contrasts. The Biblical story is known in the Hebrew tradition as the *aqedah,* from the root *'qd,* 'to bind' (to an altar), and we, too, will keep the term throughout this book. The *aqedah* constitutes a paradigm of potentially cross-cultural usefulness, whose minimal defining features are as follows: (1) The sacrifice proceeds out of a divine command *or* from a demand made on the father, implicitly or otherwise, by the metaphysical ultimate; (2) this sacrifice must have no easily recognizable or comprehensible logic, above all, no utilitarian explanation or rationale; indeed, it may seem, rather, to represent a kind of absurdity, as Kierkegaard (following Philo of Alexandria) rightly stressed for the Biblical text.[5] To understand it, one must look for a partly inaccessible, perhaps multivalent logic of motives and hidden needs, both human and divine. This rule of thumb—that if the killing serves a readily intelligible purpose, we are not dealing with the *aqedah* model—immediately rules out Agamemnon, who sacrifices Iphigenia for the sake of restoring movement to the stranded Greek fleet; similarly, Jephtah (Judges 11) and his many Greek analogues,[6] and indeed *most* stories of filicide in the world's great narrative traditions belong outside this highly specific pattern.

But what about Varuṇa and Bhṛgu? Does the sacrifice serve any commonsense goal, or bear any discursive meaning that could be formulated in ordinary language? It is, of course, linked to a ritual, that of Vedic sacrifice, which condenses the mysteries of life and death in the context of forging a connection with an ultimate truth. But let us, for the moment, put aside this question about how to classify the *Jaiminīya* text. We should note that this story belongs in a lengthy and varied series of Indian tales about parents

5. Kierkegaard ([1843] 1954); Philo, *De Abrahamo* 178; see Spiegel (1967), 9–12.

6. Such as Leos, son of Orpheus, who sacrificed his daughters to save the city from famine: see Spiegel (1967), 10.

who kill their children. Some of these parents and children (usually sons) are very famous: there is, for example, the Upaniṣadic hero Naciketas, whose father, a frustrated ritualist, sends him to a fateful encounter with Death;[7] or, again in the context of Vedic ritual, we have Śunaḥśepa, whose father cheerfully offers him as a substitute victim at another sacrificer's rite.[8] Both these latter stories seem, at least on the surface, to resemble that of Varuṇa and Bhṛgu, with which we began. Others, from the regional and folk traditions, are less well known.[9] The motif itself is extremely widespread. Often, the father's attack on his son seems to fit the "Indian Oedipal" pattern which, as A. K. Ramanujan has suggested,[10] generally reverses the direction of violence familiar to us from the Greek myth: thus in many South Indian folktales, angry fathers set out to control, dominate, and even destroy their own children. An element of sexual rivalry or jealousy may also be present, as in the Telugu tale of Sāraṅgadhara and its close analogue, the Panjabi narratives of Pūran Bhagat:[11] here the father is misled by a rejected and vindictive queen into punishing a more or less innocent son (the Phaedra-Hippolytus type). In other cases, the sacrifice serves some clear ulterior purpose, such as the parents' greed, as in a powerful riddling tale from the "Vampire" section of the *Kathāsaritsāgara;*[12] here, incidentally, as in the well-known story of Vīravara and his son Śaktidhara (also from the *Kathāsaritsāgara*),[13] the victim eagerly and consciously volunteers for the sacrifice.

One could go on listing such stories, which could no doubt easily be sorted into a rudimentary typology. All of them repay care-

7. *Kaṭha Upaniṣad;* cf. *Taittirīya Brāhmaṇa* 3.11.8.1–6; the story is retold in *MBh* 13.60 and in the Telugu *kāvya* of Dugguballi Duggana, *Nāsiketopākhyānamu.*

8. See below, chapter 4.

9. See the Panjabi story of Tārārāṇi, as summarized by Kathleen Erndl (private communication); also in Doniger (1992). Here a king sacrifices both his beloved blue horse and his son in order to receive a direct vision of the goddess. And see Mines (1984), 56.

10. Ramanujan (1983); see also Goldman (1978); Obeyesekere (1990), 71–139.

11. See discussion in Narayana Rao, Shulman, and Subrahmanyam (1992).

12. *Vetālapañcaviṃśatikā* 20 (*Kathāsaritsāgara* 94).

13. *Vetālapañcaviṃśatikā* 4(*Kathāsaritsāgara* 78) ; see Penzer's note (1924–28), 6:272–73; also *Hitopadeśa* 3, after verse 102.

ful thought and study in light of the particular contexts which produced them. But my purpose in this book is different. We will be concerned only with the rather limited subtype of Hindu tales of filicide that fit, more or less closely, the *aqedah* pattern outlined above. Hindu and not Buddhist tales—the strikingly similar story of Vessantara/Viśvantara, recorded in the *Jātaka* collections, will not be explored here.[14] We will thus be left with only a few examples, some of them perhaps so distinctive as to render their classification ambiguous (or to justify the definition of a separate subcategory, as I will eventually suggest for the late-Vedic and Upaniṣadic variants).

Let me state again our working definition and its consequences: a story of filicide in which the sacrifice is conceived in straightforward terms, and is linked to a well-articulated goal (e.g., saving the master's kingdom; building a city or a shrine; bringing relief from drought or famine) is outside our terms of reference. We are interested in the complex relations between the theme of filicide and an ultimate, perhaps ultimately unknowable, level of being, as conceived and elaborated within several specific South Asian cultural milieux.

There is a certain range of thought and feeling connected with this kind of story. The *aqedah* type normally emerges out of the interaction of some form of faith or ultimate commitment with an ambiguous, painfully internalized demand; its mode is tortuous, and profoundly open to question; often the tradition that records it also subsequently works through the strands of ambivalence and negation that constitute its inner structure. Moreover, perhaps precisely by virtue of this complex interweaving of conflicting elements in a questioning narrative form, both the Biblical and the South Indian *aqedah* materials achieve a position of obvious centrality within their cultures. Later texts resume the narrative, rework its premises, develop its paradigmatic character, so that it comes to function as what has been called a "root metaphor" for its civilization; the story's generative quality, which reflects its complexity, its power, and perhaps something of its unsettling terror, is immediately obvious by the intensity and variety of later

14. See Cone and Gombrich (1977), for discussion which also notes the relevance of the *aqedah* type.

reference, including nonliterary and nonverbal media. Our task is to trace this history as we seek to unravel the cumulating, sometimes conflicting meanings of the Hindu *aqedah*.

We will concentrate on three stories: first, the Tamil tale of the Little Devotee, in its earliest complete telling and in its development through the medieval Telugu tradition (chapters 2 and 3); then, plunging back through time and the sources, the Vedic instance of Rohita and Śunaḥśepa (chapter 4); finally, the unusual Upaniṣadic type seen in the story of Śuka and Vyāsa, from the Sanskrit epic (chapter 5). This order, clearly antichronological, should be briefly explained: the Tamil/Telugu tale is, at least formally and superficially, the closest Indian parallel to the Biblical paradigm (both in the structure of the story and in its rich development by the exegetical tradition); it therefore seemed best to begin with these materials, which are also, like the Biblical account, informed by a powerful, if implicit, theology. On the other hand, the distinctiveness of the Upaniṣadic or "gnostic" type emerges most clearly, and naturally, out of its Vedic antecedents (the Śunaḥśepa story); and here the contrast with the South Indian, theistic *aqedah* is particularly illuminating. I hope to trace a certain contrastive logic underlying these typological divisions, and relating to central issues of symbolization, literalization, paradoxicality, and the claims of knowledge; these issues are thrown into relief as we move from the relatively familiar world of South Indian devotionalism, with its passionate poses, into the more ancient realms of Vedic ritual and the Upaniṣadic hunger for release. The logic of types also incorporates an essential differentiation in the notion of sacrifice, as we will see. The sequence of the argument is again outlined in the final summary, which tries to draw these threads together, at the same time reformulating their separate and particular character.

The Biblical *aqedah,* with which we began, may claim a certain latent presence in our discussions; in the concluding chapter, this presence is foregrounded in a comparative mode. Moreover, having excluded, on principle, the Greek Iphigenia cycle, I can now reintroduce it as the classical "other," an illuminating foil especially to the Vedic variants of our major type. Indeed, the classical resonances set off by the Hindu materials are much too precious to be ignored, and we will several times find ourselves drifting happily into surprising juxtapositions. I assume, as a working hypothesis, that each of the stories presents us with a unique vision, with highly specific conceptual and symbolic elements requiring explication; and also that such explication may be sharpened by competing memories from other, perhaps more familiar texts.

We have, then, an initial frame, perhaps already a little too rigidly defined. We are interested in the Indian *aqedah* types, following Philo's lead. This definition has the great advantage of limiting the field to a certain workable range. Before entering fully into this arena, however, I want to look at one more story, from somewhere on the boundary of our classification—a story which thus illuminates that boundary and sets the tone for the first major text to come. Indeed, this is a story taken from that same Tamil text, the *Pĕriya Purāṇam (PP),* that offers the earliest version of the sacrifice performed by the Little Devotee, our prime exemplar of the South Indian *aqedah*. We are, then, already close to the center of our concern. This text, the twelfth-century compilation of Śaiva hagiographies by Cekkiḻār (a court poet for the Chola king Kulottuṅga II), begins with its own frame-story relating to the ancient town of Tiruvārūr in the Kāverī Delta:

In Tiruvārūr reigned Maṉunīticoḻaṉ, a righteous king who had performed countless sacrifices, and who had named himself after the true "rules of Manu."[15] He worshiped according to proper rite the god who dwells in the anthill,[16] who is everywhere. Because of the king's goodness and ascetic restraint, a son was born to him—a wonderful boy who, as he grew, learned all the sacred arts that bring one close to God *(civam),* as well as the practical wisdom of riding horses and elephants and driving chariots. In his case, it was as if existence itself, though brought about through the deadly deeds of previous lives, was a gift.

One day, when the boy was close to being made Crown Prince, he went for a ride through the town in his chariot. Drums were beating, the bards and panegyrists were singing his praises, and all the women who saw him at once fell in love with him and grew

15. I.e., the laws of dharma, as encoded in the *Mānavadharmaśāstra*.

16. Valmīkanātha, Śiva at the great temple in Tiruvārūr, where the central *liṅga* (sign of Siva) rises from an anthill.

thin with longing, so that their bangles slid off their arms into the streets he passed. Suddenly—as if Dharma itself wished to test, in a merciless manner, the true nature of the king's mind *(paṉippil cintaiyiṉil uṇmaip pāṉmai cotittāl ĕṉṉa)*—a young, almost newborn calf wandered unsteadily into the street and, before anyone could see or stop it, was crushed to death under the wheels of the chariot.

The mother cow saw this happen and broke into painful cries of sorrow. The prince, aware that a disaster had taken place, hardly able to speak, his heart broken, came down from the chariot and looked at the mother and her child. "I was born to bring hitherto unknown disgrace *(paḻi)* upon my father, the king," he said; "my awareness *(uṇarvu)* has been wholly destroyed; what am I to do?" Then he thought: "Perhaps *dharma* is to act in this case according to the instructions of the Brahmins, versed in the Vedas, who can do away with this disgrace. I will seek them out before my father hears of this." And he hastened away.

The mother cow, tears pouring from her eyes, stumbled painfully toward the palace of the king. There, at the entrance, hung a bell, which anyone could ring to summon the king to give judgment; the cow rang the bell with her horns. This unknown sound—the drumbeat of disgrace? the sound of binding evil? the bell on the neck of Yama's buffalo, as the Lord of Death approached to take the prince's life?—reached the ears of the king, and he at once came down from his throne and hastened to the palace gate. When he saw the cow, he angrily asked his ministers what had happened, and one of them, who already knew the story, bowed at his master's feet and briefly informed him of the accident.

The king felt at once the whole grief suffered by the cow *(āv uṟu tuyaram ĕyti);* his inner being was suffused by pain, as if poison had reached his head. "How did this happen?" he cried; "this is a beautiful instance of my righteous rule *(cĕvvit' ĕṉ cĕṅkol ĕṉṉum)*."

His ministers responded: "Mental weakness on your part will not solve the problem. The dharmic answer is to prescribe for your son the penance laid down by the Vedic Brahmins for the slaughter of a cow."

Now the king was indignant: "Will the way you have indicated bring any solace to the cow? You are afraid I am going to lose my son. But will not dharma turn away in disgust if I agree to this evil course *(caḻakku)* you have outlined? A king must protect his subjects from any obstacles coming from himself, his associates, his enemies, thieves, or any other living being. That is dharma! If I let my son perform penance to rid himself of this evil, and then, when someone else commits a murder, I prescribe the death penalty for him, I, King Manu, will wipe out the chain that goes back to Manu's ancient book."

"But," objected the ministers, "this is how the world has always behaved. It is not right to execute your son. The right way is to keep to the dharma described in the Veda."

"You are talking rubbish," cried the king, his face red as a lotus dipped in flame. "You have no thought for the truth that lies in the dharmic way. You tell me: *what* cow, in *what* world, came, grieving, to *whose* door? My son killed a living being born in Tiruvārūr, where Śiva lives;[17] therefore, he must die. I am unable to remove the sorrow that has taken over the mind of that cow; the only way for me to act *(karumam)* is thus to ensure that I suffer myself the same grief *she* feels."

He summoned his son and ordered one of the ministers to take him into the street and drive his chariot over him. The minister could not do it; he killed himself instead. So the king himself placed his son under the wheel and drove the chariot over his heart.

Is it difficult—so Cekkiḻār, the narrator-poet, asks rhetorically, as he reaches the climax of his story—is it difficult, or is it easy to be a king?

No one who witnessed this deed could bear it—not the people of this world, whose tears poured out like torrents of rain; nor the gods in heaven, who rained down flowers; not even Śiva, who is Vītiviṭaṅkappĕrumāṉ, the Lovely Lord of the Street in Tiruvārūr. He came rushing into that street, riding his bull, with the goddess taking up the left half of his body, his troops of demons on either side. The calf, the prince, and the dead minister all stood up. But the king hardly grasped what had happened. When God stands

17. A reference to the belief that mere birth in Tiruvārūr is enough to bring one to release (like dying in Benares, or seeing Cidambaram). To kill someone who has won the privilege of being born in Tiruvārūr is thus an extraordinary form of evil.

before you, is there anything that cannot be? The father embraced his son, the calf nursed at its mother's teats, milk soaked the dusty earth of Tiruvārūr.[18]

Is this a story of the *aqedah* type? Strictly speaking, surely not—the sacrifice serves the obvious purpose of punishing the prince for his accidental act of murder, and maintaining the king's unblemished record of righteous rule. In this latter respect, we should note a slight wavering in the text's perspective on the rules of Manu, which give this king his name; clearly, the Brahmins, no less faithful to these rules than the king, could have found a way out of the dilemma without demanding the prince's life. Thus, though we know this king as Maṉunītikaṇṭacoḻaṉ, "the Chola who observed Manu's code," in effect he goes well beyond the letter of the law in the name of a higher vision. It is this vision, and its emotional and metaphysical motivations, that we need to address.

When we do so, we find ourselves surprisingly close to the *aqedah*. Notice, for one thing, the theme of testing that is said to underlie the whole tragic incident: it is "as if Dharma itself wished to test, in a merciless manner, the true nature of the king's mind." Still, the sacrifice is articulated in terms of its own logic, the test being entirely hidden from the king. He acts not out of calculation or self-interest—although he is clearly aware of the perverse example he could set by letting his son atone through penance, whereas other killers would pay with their lives (and thus a somewhat exotic egalitarianism creeps into this king's reading of Manu's code!). Rather, he is primarily motivated by a profound empathy with the bereaved mother. When he first hears the story, the king feels in himself "the whole grief suffered by the cow"; this sorrow completely takes over his mind, overriding any other thought or emotion, including, of course, his ministers' well-meaning, politically sensible plan; in the end, it is this same empathy that provides the clinching argument for the execution: "the only way for me to act is thus to ensure that I suffer myself the same grief *she* feels." This is a cry from the heart: the Chola assumes responsibility for all his subjects' suffering, which he internalizes, to devastating effect; his means of living out this responsi-

18. *PP* 1.3.13–50 (my summary).

bility is to force himself to feel precisely what *they* feel, as if this sharing of emotion were, in itself, the quintessential mode of being true.

This is very much a Tamil psychology of interaction. What counts is, first and foremost, the inner emotional reality, which abrogates the normative divisions between living beings. Shared sensation, especially of great intensity—especially sensation focused on or derived from loss and separation—becomes a form of self-transcendence. Tamil often refers to such experiences as "melting," "liquefaction" (*urukkam, urukutal*—and, indeed, this verb [*uruku*] is present in the telling of this tale, with reference to the cow's mourning).[19] The king, taken over by another's grief, loses himself in a movement of real metaphysical impact; he also establishes or confirms a paradigm by this response, thus transforming, on some level, the reality of his kingdom and creating the conditions for contact with divinity. By letting himself know the other's sorrow, and acting on this knowledge, the king ultimately produces the god's revelation in the dusty street.

Two elements are crucial to this progression. First, it is clearly not enough for the king to achieve a state of merely imaginative empathy or identification with the suffering cow; having internalized the emotion initially, he is still driven in the direction of a concrete *externalization* in action, that takes the form of sacrifice. Everything depends on the intensity of the sensation, but this, in turn, seems to depend upon a real event enacted in the world; this king must know the cow's experience by reexperiencing it on his own terms, by undergoing a directly analogous loss. The movement thus is from external event to shared, internal emotion to another externalized action. The emotional linkage demands an outer revelation. Second, this sequence is resumed on a more encompassing level with reference to the god, who witnesses these events from the local temple.[20] It appears that the king's internali-

19. On *urukkam* or *urukutal,* see Trawick [Egnor] (1978), 19–21; also Narayana Rao, Ramanujan, and Shulman (in press). Here, v. 23/108, *uruku tāy.* Other verbs of overpowering, painful emotion—*coru, iraṅku, vĕmpiṭu, taḷaru, uyir, alaṟu, eṅku, tĕrumaru, iṭar uṟu*—which recur in this passage are also intimately linked to devotional contexts, and to the emotions that come to the fore when the Tamil person thinks of god.

20. I am grateful to Yonah Shahar-Levi for pointing this out to me.

zation of his subject's grief and the consequent enactment of this sensation in further sacrifice is meant to work upon the god in a similar manner: Śiva now, for his part, cannot bear to feel *his* subject's suffering, as the text explicitly states. The god, too, is swept along by the painful empathy that demolishes boundaries and connects all actors to a deeper truth. He, too, must act, to move the dead back across the line dividing them from the living, so that the escalating cycles of loss can come to a temporary halt. Sacrifice, reversed, ends in images of nurturing care: the father embraces the son he so recently executed; the calf, and the everyday street where all this has taken place, are bathed in milk; the god, perfectly visible in this same street, this familiar human and animal world, looks benignly on. We know that he, too, has been strangely moved.

It is important to realize that on this level, the surface rationale of the sacrifice loses its importance, almost to the point of utter meaninglessness. True, the king has upheld the binding (and universal) power of the law—although, in fact, as already noted, he has exceeded its demands. True, the prince has atoned for his unwitting "crime" by undergoing a symmetrical punishment, as the king has expiated *his* responsibility by suffering a precisely symmetrical sorrow. True, the king's righteousness has been splendidly affirmed, so that future generations will recall his deed with awe and, in the case of his Chola successors, with pride at being in his lineage.[21] Yet none of this really affects the core sequence we have outlined. What really matters is not the calculus of evil and its expiation—indeed, it is this calculated modality that the king abhors in the code of penances to which his ministers refer him—but the emotional logic of identification, self-transcendence, and the achievement of ultimacy. On this level, the "trial" instigated

21. Thus Maṉunītikaṇṭacoḻaṉ assumes a role of importance in the Chola genealogies; Cekkiḻār himself makes reference to this by associating *his* patron, Anapāyaṉ (= Kulottuṅga) with this model (1.3.13). Cf. *Cilappatikāram* 20.53–55; *Maṇimekalai* 22.210; *Kaliṅkattupparaṇi* 187; the story is also known in the Sri Lankan tradition. In the passage from *Cilappatikāram,* Maṉunītikaṇṭacoḻaṉ is paired with Śibi, the king who offered his own flesh in place of a dove, as known from the *Jātakas;* the Cholas also claimed Śibi as an ancestor. It is possible that our story is also rooted in a Buddhist milieu; still, in Cekkiḻār's telling, already prefigured by the brief reference in *Cilappatikāram* to the empathy motif, it has acquired a characteristically Tamil coloring.

by Dharma is a means of establishing connection with the god, through the medium of feeling and sensation where his presence is most readily at hand. The Chola's act of murderous self-abnegation, at base, more an act of solidarity than of renunciation, coerces this divine presence into palpable, sensory revelation and dramatic action. We might even suspect that, in some sense, the story speaks to the existence of a divine need for just this type of experience, for revelation elicited by a relationship articulated through strong human feeling, of a predominantly painful and violent tone.

Before concluding this discussion, we need to reexamine one critical term. I have used the word "sacrifice" rather loosely, without attempting a definition. Clearly, however, we must distinguish the form of offering described here from the classical Brahminical system of sacrifice usually referred to as *yajña*.[22] The latter proceeds through elaborate technical procedures, encoded in the *Brāhmaṇa* and other ritual texts, and reflects a metaphysics of dense symbolic equations and correspondences, which allow for movement between planes of reality. We will have more to say about this kind of sacrifice in chapter 4. By way of contrast, our story presents us with a type inimical to symbolism: only the literal enactment of violent loss, on the level of primitive experience, is effective here. Indeed, such literalization is actually the exact opposite of symbolization, as we see by the king's refusal to consider any form of substitution for his son. Throughout the *Pĕriya Purāṇam,* such acts of literal surrender are extravagantly praised and preferred. In effect, what is required is the sacrifice of some part or parts of the self—always in a literal, nonsymbolic mode, which is perceived as touching the deepest, most fundamental level of experience. The king, by internalizing against himself the cow's primitive desire for revenge, successfully acts out this type of sacrifice. Henceforth, in discussing the South Indian texts, it is this meaning of the term that should be kept in mind. It is remarkable that this form of literalized offering of the self, from within the

22. In Tamil, the corresponding term to *yajña* is often *veḷvi,* from the root *veḷ,* "to offer sacrifice; to marry; to desire" (*DED* 4561). The last meaning is crucial to the historical semantics of this word. Sacrifice, including Vedic sacrifice, has, in Tamil, overtones of love and desire. We will explore this notion further with reference to the second type of sacrifice, defined below.

self, also operates on the god, who thereby brings into play a liberating "downward transcendence."[23] In general, the direction in our story is "downward," in this sense—away from symbolism, even, perhaps, from cognition and conceptualization, toward unmediated emotion and the uncompromising, literal self-sacrifice that proceeds from such a stance.

These themes will occupy us at length below in the context of a story more directly defined within the main *aqedah* pattern. It remains striking that the frame of our text includes the following notions: the metaphysical power of overriding emotion; the twofold transition between inner and outer domains, as feeling spills into action, and vice versa; the apparent necessity for externalization of this sort in the context of experiencing truth; the relation of empathy and emotional identification to deeds of violent "sacrifice," in the sense just noted; the efficacy of such sacrifice in triggering the god's revelation; the complicated motivational structure within which such revelation can take place. We have moved away, far away, from the kind of offering that is simply meant to fulfill some concrete, predetermined need. We are already amazingly close to a world where the god can demand, and receive, a gift of ultimate horror offered in love.

23. I am indebted to A. K. Ramanujan for this term, and for clarifying the distinction between these forms of sacrifice.

2

The Little Devotee according to Cekkiḻār

And what meaning would we have
if he, whom we long for,
had already been?

—Rilke

1

The name of Ciṟuttŏṇṭar, the Little Devotee from the village of Tiruccĕṅkāṭṭaṅkuṭi in the Kāverī Delta, was known to Tiruñāṉa-campantar and Cuntaramūrtti, the *Tevāram* poets (seventh and ninth centuries, respectively); but his story, as we have it, is first elaborated in Chola-period Tamil sources.[1] Nampi Āṇṭār Nampi, probably in the tenth century, tells us that

famous Ciṟuttŏṇṭar destroyed the power of the Kali Age
by cutting up the body of his only son
  with his sweet lisp,
  bells chiming on his feet,
and offering him as ambrosia *(amutu)*

1. Cuntarar's *Tiruttŏṇṭattŏkai,* the first complete listing of the 63 Śaiva saints (early ninth-century?), mentions "Ciṟuttŏṇṭaṉ who dwelled in Cĕṅkāṭṭaṅkuṭi" (39.6/398), a formula familiar from Tiruñāṉacampantar as well; there is no hint of the gruesome story. By the early eleventh century, an inscription from this village speaks of a festival in honor of Ciṟuttŏṇṭanampi, who worshiped Śiva in the forms of Mahādeva-Sīrāḷadeva and Vīrabhadra—the latter to be identified, perhaps, with the dread Bhairava mentioned in Cekkiḻār's text. (SII II, app. C, 59.) For an overview of the Tamil tradition on Ciṟuttŏṇṭar, see Dorai Rangaswamy (1959), 1009–19; and the interpretative essay by Hart (1979), with translation of Cekkiḻār's version.

to the god who wears
a tiger's skin.[2]

Clearly, the lineaments of the tale, and even parts of its specific vocabulary, were already in place. Yet even if we assume, as we no doubt should, that the story was fully formed long before Cekkiḻār recorded it in the mid-twelfth century in his *Tiruttŏṇṭar Purāṇam* or *Pĕriya Purāṇam (PP),* it is this text, the earliest complete version and unquestionably one of the most eloquent, that has become its *locus classicus* (*PP* 7.3.1–88). It is only natural, then, that we start with Cekkiḻār and his poem.

Let me preface a few words about the *Pĕriya Purāṇam* generally and its place within the Tamil Śaiva world. Tradition tells us that the author composed his monumental work in order to divert the king's attention from a Jaina Tamil *kāvya* (the *Cīvakacintāmaṇi; kāvya* refers to a long narrative poem in elevated style); and, indeed, this is entirely a Tamil Hindu work, reflecting the values of South Indian Śaivism as embodied in extreme, often melodramatic narrative form, as we saw above, in the case of Maṉunītikaṇṭacoḻaṉ. Its stories are usually rather grisly, rich in pathos and violent demonstrations of fanatical devotion to the god—and none more so than the tale of the Little Devotee; as such, they may perhaps be seen more as paradigmatic than as normative, although the later tradition often struggles bitterly with these prestigious models.

Cekkiḻār was active at a moment when the Tamil Śaiva tradition was busy crystallizing and arranging the various textual, legendary, and ritual traditions that had been created over the previous five centuries or so, since the time of the early *Nāyaṉmār* poet-saints; hagiography, especially in a mode which sought to contextualize each surviving poem from the Śaiva *bhakti* corpus, was a major element in this more encompassing endeavor, hence the comprehensive character of Cekkiḻār's work. In purely poetic terms, the *Pĕriya Purāṇam* is surpassed by Kampaṉ's *Irāmāvatāram,* the other great *kāvya* from the middle Chola period; but as an expression of the psychology and metaphysics of Tamil devotional religion, at least in its Śaiva variant, Cekkiḻār's encyclopedic

2. *Tiruttŏṇṭar tiruvantāti* 43.

hagiography has no equal. It is primarily on this level that we wish to explore what is surely the most problematic of all his tales.

There is something else to be kept in mind as we read the *Pĕriya Purāṇam*. Cekkiḻār was a Veḷāḷa, that is, a high-caste nonBrahmin from a caste associated primarily with paddy cultivation. The Veḷāḷas and allied agricultural castes had always provided the essential backbone for institutionalized Śaivism in the Tamil country (as, indeed, they might be said largely to have sustained the traditional social order generally, with its political and religious institutions). In terms of the usual South Indian metaphor, this is a "right-hand" group deeply linked to the land, hence to a sedentary life-style and culturally conservative tendencies.[3] In South India, such land-bound groups often generated texts of a pronounced "martial" quality, keyed, perhaps, to the perception of agriculture as inherently violent and to the struggle for possession of the land.[4] The gory stories of Tamil Śaivism thus emerge logically out of a specific social context; one of our concerns in the following pages will be to trace the transformations that resulted from the appropriation of these stories by other contexts, other cultural worlds. The Little Devotee provides us, by virtue of his centrality and evocative power, with a perfect test case for this problem.

Now let us see how Cekkiḻār tells the tale.

2

We meet our hero, Ciṟuttŏṇṭar, under another name—Parañcoti, of the great Māmāttirar clan devoted to protecting all living beings. He is, thus, a warrior, and as such he serves his king in the famous battle for Vātāpi.[5] When the king discovers that this hero is a devotee of Śiva, and has been exposed to danger in the royal service, he is mortified and seeks Parañcoti's forgiveness; but the latter humbly remarks that he has simply been performing his proper work *(ĕṉ urimai tŏḻil)*, and there is surely no harm in that. The king sends him home loaded down with honors and riches. Note that in this brief introduction, seemingly quite separate from

3. See Shulman (1992b), and literature cited there.

4. Narayana Rao (1986).

5. On the dating of this Pallava campaign, see Dorai Rangaswamy (1959), 1015–17.

the main narrative of horrific sacrifice, the hero's native affinity with violence is directly stated.

Back in the village of Cĕṅkāṭṭaṅkuṭi, Parañcoti marries Vĕṇkāṭṭunaṅkai and lives the proper, dharmic life of the householder. His major concern is with feeding the Śaiva devotees: he eats only after he has found some of them to feed; and because of this constant, humble service, he becomes known as Ciṟuttŏṇṭar, the "Little Devotee." In the course of time, a son, Cīrāḷaṉ, is born to the couple, to the father's immense joy.

Five years pass. The child is already in school, learning "clarity of speech that flowers into thought." Ciṟuttŏṇṭar's special form of service has reached the feet of Śiva on Kailāsa, and the god, "in order to savor the love that has the essence of truth" (*mĕyttaṉmaiy aṉpu nukarnt' aruḷutaṟku,* 25), comes down to earth in the form of an extreme Śaiva ascetic, a Bhairava *(vairavar).* This is a crucial statement, the only time the text directly approaches the question "why" in relation to the story it narrates; the answer has nothing to do with a test or trial, but everything to do with the experiencing of real emotion. The god's disguise is minutely, and somewhat playfully, described: the crescent moon in his hair becomes, as it were, a forehead mark *(pŏṭṭu)* of gleaming white ash; a necklace of brilliant crystal hides the dark stain on his throat (left over from the time he swallowed the ocean's black poison); the flayed skin of the elephant-demon, Gajāsura, covers his body, red as coral, as darkness engulfs the red horizon at sunset. He is draped in garlands and necklaces, "as if the love of the devotees had taken bodily form." His left hand holds the trident and Brahmā's skull, his right the *tamarukam* drum. And he is smiling—a compassionate smile, soothing as moonlight (even as the trident, enemy of evil, seems to emit burning sunlight). We must not lose sight of this smile, especially as the tale enters into its horrific phase; Śiva has come to demand a sacrifice—the ultimate sacrifice—but he does so with a smile, and in disguise. He is dressed to imitate a Bhairava ascetic who, naturally, imitates the god himself, with all his iconic attributes; this is, then, a double mimesis, Śiva posing as a living, human replica of himself. The demand he makes will thus be mediated, at least in part, by the assumed human voice that speaks for, or in place of, the god in all his fullness and distance. By the same token, the god's presence in this story enacts a conscious, deliberate movement in the direction of human emotion and experience.

In the above guise, Śiva arrives in Cĕṅkāṭṭaṅkuṭi in the Tamil land. He is as if in the grip of a terrible hunger, an insatiable desire *(taṇṭāta ŏru veṭkaip paciy uṭaiyār tamaip pola)*. He asks the way to the home of the Little Devotee. But Ciṟuttŏṇṭar is not in, as the maidservant, Cantaṉattār, informs the visitor: the master of the house has gone looking for Śaiva devotees to feed. Ciṟuttŏṇṭar's wife, Vĕṇkāṭṭammai, afraid that this newfound guest will disappear, begs him to come in and wait. The ascetic, however, refuses: he will not remain alone with women in a house. He is, he tells them, from the North *(uttarāpatiy uḷḷom)*, and he has come to see the Little Devotee; he will wait for him under the *ātti* tree in Śiva's shrine of Kaṇapatīccaram, in the village.

When Ciṟuttŏṇṭar returns—in despair at having found no one to feed—his wife tells him the happy news. "I am saved!" cries the devotee, as he rushes to bow to the ascetic under the *ātti* tree. "Are you the great Little Devotee?" asks the Bhairava, toying with the oxymoron, and Ciṟuttŏṇṭar admits that he has been given this name; he also speaks of his frustration: "In my desire *(kātalāle)*, I went searching through this village for someone to feed, but saw no one; now, through my *tapas*, I have discovered you. You must eat in your servant's home."

A somewhat eery dialogue, rich in veiled double entendres, ensues:

Ascetic: We have come to see you. We are from the North. But you cannot feed us, for all your love; it is an impossible deed.

Ciṟuttŏṇṭar: I have not spoken without thought. Tell me how to make your food. Nothing is impossible, nothing too difficult when the devotees of Śiva are concerned.

Ascetic: You are filled with love. When three seasons have passed, the day comes to slay a beast *(pacu)* for our food; today is that day. You see you cannot feed us.

Ciṟuttŏṇṭar: Excellent! I have three kinds of herds. You are devoted to the god who swallowed poison: just tell me what kind of beast you want, and I will quickly prepare it, before the proper moment passes.

Ascetic: The beast we eat is human. It must be five years old, without blemish. And there is one thing more I must tell you, like thrusting a lance into a painful wound.

Ciṟuttŏṇṭar: Nothing is too difficult; please have mercy and speak.

Ascetic: It must be a good, only son of a good family. The father must cut him as the mother holds him, as their hearts rejoice. That is the curry we shall eat.

Ciṟuttŏṇṭar remains undaunted:

"Even this is not hard—
if only our lord will agree to eat."
He spoke quickly,
savoring the joy,
in passion
as he bowed at the feet
   tender as the honey-filled lotus
and hurried home. (52)

Is this the same passion *(kātal)* that has driven him to search all day for at least a single guest? The one who has so mysteriously materialized is clearly too precious to be lost, and Ciṟuttŏṇṭar takes upon himself, willingly and seemingly without reflection, the whole burden of his outlandish request. He cannot hear the ironic overtones of his visitor's statements: the god is, after all, correct in stating that no one, not even this fanatical feeder, can truly appease his hunger. As so often in texts of the South Indian devotional traditions, divine speech is surprisingly literal and precise, although its human audience fails to comprehend the message on this level; Ciṟuttŏṇṭar must assume that his guest is simply being coy, hesitant, or polite. He meets this ambiguous negotiation with a fundamental simplicity of surrender; the guest is a Śaiva, and, as such, a living form of his god, who commands love, self-sacrifice, service. Desire, articulated in these terms, pervades the human situation and determines the Little Devotee's response.

So he rushes home to inform his wife. He breaks the news gently, in a verse whose staggered syntax beautifully reflects the escalating strangeness and horror of this moment:

The great ascetic who came here
has agreed to eat with us, with a happy heart—
if it is a family's only son,

a boy of five years,
flawless in all his limbs,
a child
to be held in joy by his mother,
slain in joy by the father,
and cooked for this meal.[6] (54)

The climax in the original occurs at the start of the fourth line—usually the point of greatest tension in a Tamil verse—with the head-rhyming *piḷḷai,* "a child," that is the proper focus of the request, which is properly phrased in the conditional. There is room here for a choice, as the "if" makes clear. As throughout this unnerving text, the patent horror is rendered starker by the explicit and recurrent insistence on joyfulness. In a way, this is the most extreme demand of all—not simply that the sacrifice be carried out, but that its executors act in joy. The mother now briefly balks, understandably refusing to understand: "We will make this meal, but how are we to find such a child?" Ciṟuttŏṇṭar, of course, is ready with the answer:

He looked straight in her eyes.
"Even if one were to offer
a great treasure, to the heart's content,
who would give such a child?
No father and mother would stand there
and slaughter their own son.
There is no time to be lost
if *I* am to be saved:
the boy that you brought forth
is the one we must call." (56)

She agrees; her husband goes to bring the child home from school. He feels, we are told, "like someone who has attained a perfect gift." (What is this gift, if not the opportunity to offer that which he loves best?) The boy comes running to his father, who carries him home on his shoulder; his mother receives him, fusses over him—wiping his face, combing his hair, straightening his clothes—before returning him to Ciṟuttŏṇṭar. Afraid lest this

6. . . . *vanta mātavar tam/ uḷḷa'makiḻav amutu cĕyyav icaintār kuṭikk'or ciṟuvaṉumāyk/ kŏllum pirāyam aint' uḷaṉāy uṟuppiṟ kuṟaipāṭ'iṉṟit tāy/ piḷḷai piṭikkav uvantu pitāv arintu camaikkap pĕṟiṉ ĕṉṟār.*

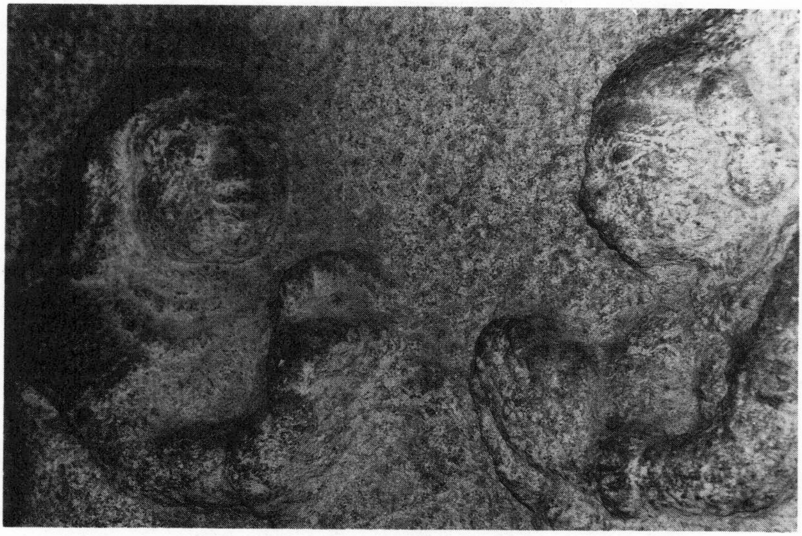

The Little Devotee informs his wife that they must sacrifice their son. Lepakshi, Andhra Pradesh. Photo: courtesy Yigal Bronner.

The child-victim is carried home from school. Lepakshi, Andhra Pradesh. Photo: courtesy Yigal Bronner.

child, soon to be turned into curry, will be polluted by his saliva, the father refrains from kissing him or even embracing him. The mother washes the necessary pots and utensils. In some secret place—so that the world will not know—the two parents, whose minds are one, prepare for the sacrifice. Vĕṇkāṭṭunaṅkai holds the boy's feet and hands, Ciṟuttŏṇṭar grips his head; now Cīrāḷaṉ, the child himself, noticing his parents' joyfulness, laughs in happiness as well. This is the moment when the father cuts off his son's head.

Again, with excruciating insistence, the poet stresses the parents' joy:

> The father was thinking, radiant
> with happiness, "My great,
> incomparable son has given us
> the essence of truth,"[7]
> and his wife thought, "My husband
> has given me precious life."
> Her inner being opened fully
> like a bud.
> Together, they exulted
> at heart, performing
> that difficult deed. (64)

So, even with the great inner softening and unfolding, it remains, on some level, a difficult deed *(ariya viṉai)*, followed now by the preparation of the meat curries and other dishes, which are elaborately described. A small detail is stressed: the parents believe that the child's head is unsuitable for this meal, and put it aside (the maidservant, Cantaṉattār, takes it away). When all is ready, Ciṟuttŏṇṭar—"thrilling with joy and desire even greater than before"—goes to summon the ascetic from under the *ātti* tree.

He apologizes for the delay: the guest must surely be hungry *(pacitt' aruḷa)*. He leads him home, offers him a seat, washes his feet, and sprinkles the water thus purified over himself and his wife. The house is filled with fragrant flowers and incense lamps, and the couple, treating their guest as a god, perform *pūjā* before

7. *mĕyttaṉmai:* see above, when Śiva initiates this entire episode in order to experience "the love that has the essence of truth" (*mĕyttaṉmaiy aṉpu,* 25). The essential truth to be demonstrated and experienced seems integrally connected to this form of sacrifice.

Ciṟuttŏṇṭar and Vĕṇkāṭṭunaṅkai sacrifice their son. On the right: the maidservant Cantaṉattār receives the boy's head. In the upper left: the disguised Bhairava-Śiva under the *ātti* tree in the temple courtyard. South Indian etching. Photo: courtesy Dennis Hudson.

him. They receive his permission to serve the meal. But first he inquires: "Have you made curries from all the parts of the animal, as you were told?" Ciṟuttŏṇṭar has to confess: "My wife felt the head would not be proper food, and put it aside." "I will eat that, too," says the ascetic, in the first of a new series of teasing, exasperating demands.

Ciṟuttŏṇṭar and his wife are in a panic, their thoughts confused. Fortunately, the maidservant has made a curry from the head as well, just in case. Disaster has been averted. But again the guest looks at Ciṟuttŏṇṭar and says, "I cannot eat alone. There must be some devotees standing somewhere near; bring them here." Another moment of panic—another obstacle to the feast. Ciṟuttŏṇṭar races outside to look, one last time, for another guest. There is, of course, no one. Wearily, he returns to face the Bhairava ascetic: "I see no one here or elsewhere; but I, myself, follow the way of those who cover themselves in sacred ash."

"Then you shall eat with me," commands the god. The food is served. Ciṟuttŏṇṭar is ready even for this: his overriding concern is with bringing his guest to the point of eating. So he, the father, reaches out to partake of the grisly meal. At the last moment, the Bhairava stops him with yet another unexpected demand. "We eat once in six months. You never miss a meal. Why are you rushing to eat first? Call your flawless son to join us."

Is this not a terrible mockery of the sacrifice? The guest is tormenting his host, forcing him beyond the limits of sanity. What is left for the Little Devotee? He has offered up his son; he has held nothing back; he has given himself over completely to the required joy of single-hearted devotion. A moment before, he was preparing to join the cannibalistic feast. This latest demand finally destroys any residual logic adhering to the deed—even if we assume, as Ciṟuttŏṇṭar is, perhaps, meant to do, that the ascetic could be unaware of the identity of the sacrificial victim. From the father's point of view, it is finally too much. "He (my son) can no longer help us," he answers in despair. But the guest is relentless: "We will eat here only if he comes. Go call him." The Little Devotee thinks to himself: "What can I do to make this man eat?" The problem seems insuperable. Taking his wife, he goes outside. And, against all reason and judgment, he calls out: "Come, my son." "Come, my brilliant gem, Cīrāḷaṉ," calls the mother, a little more warmly; "this devotee of Śiva calls you to eat with him, so that we all may be saved."

Suddenly, out of nowhere:

> By the graciousness of God,
> as if running home from school,
> he appeared—
>   a son beautiful
>   beyond compare.
> She took him in her arms,
> caressed him with her hands,
> gave him to her husband
> in sharp, surpassing joy—
> for, so she thought,
> that devotee of the Lord
>   who once burned the demons' Triple City[8]
> would eat at last. (82)

With the boy in his arms, the father rushes into the house; he, too, has but one thought, that is, that the tormenting guest will finally begin to eat. As the text tell us, it is this hope, and not simply the

8. Śiva destroyed the three flying cities of the demons by a fiery laugh. The wife still perceives her Bhairava-guest as a devotee of Śiva.

return of the slaughtered child, that nourishes the reborn sensation of joy. But the man has gone, and the fresh curries have also disappeared. Ciṟuttŏṇṭar is distraught, afraid, bewildered. As always, the moment of revelation is first one of loss and hiding; one discovers the god has been present only by a sudden absence. Ciṟuttŏṇṭar goes back outside. Now Śiva can show himself in his divine form, no longer masquerading as his own human imitator and image. He is there in the sky, with Pārvatī and *his* son Skanda, on the bull Nandin. He looks with compassion *(karuṇai)* at Ciṟuttŏṇṭar, his wife and son. But they, meanwhile, have melted, in their bones and hearts; they will never be separated from God again.

3

Surface Features

So the sacrifice is restored, and the entire family transfigured and saved, or, to use the Tamil phrase (already encountered in the story of the Chola king), melted down, liquefied in an emotional flooding of such intensity that, so the poet states, the very possibility of separation of any kind is henceforth precluded. The revelation caps the process of outrageous demand, with its escalating, tantalizing momentum, and also justifies the Little Devotee's selfless gift: here, as elsewhere, one has to give all in order to receive all. In this basic respect, Ciṟuttŏṇṭar and Abraham are very alike. In other respects, however, the stories diverge radically, most perspicuously, no doubt, in the simple fact that Ciṟuttŏṇṭar actually goes through with the horrendous sacrifice, while Abraham is prevented at the last minute from doing so by the angel's voice.

But let us limit ourselves, for now, to the Tamil tale. On the simplest, most overt level, of course, this is a story of radical devotion and surrender, seen as in some sense paradigmatic; love of god cannot deny—indeed, must eventually bring to pass—the most precious offering of all. Ciṟuttŏṇṭar traces a kind of limit and thereby serves as an extreme model which others may imitate from afar. Still, the centrality of this story within the southern tradition seems to derive from other, deeper currents that have molded its many tellings; and it is important to remember that even as a tale of devotion drawn out to its logical conclusion, this sacrifice remains imbued with the peculiar horror of the apparently absurd.

Does Śiva really have to demand precisely this dreadful gift? How are we to understand such a demand? As we shall see, the southern Śaiva sources themselves gravitate to these questions. One possible rationale has to be excluded from the start, at least with reference to Cekkiḻār's version: as already stated, at no point in the Tamil text is the notion of testing the devotee even intimated; the god apparently has another purpose in mind, insofar as we can speak of a divine intention at all, in this context. In fact, more than intentionality, we seem to have here an overpowering drive or passion working within the deity, pushing him outwards toward the devotee. It is the nature of this interaction, seen in light of the complex motivations and internal forces on either side, that forms the central problem for our analysis.

We will proceed as follows: first, some remarks on the texture of Cekkiḻār's poetry, and its metaphysical implications; then an outline of the symbolism of movement and space in this story, in relation to the theme of hunger and eating; we then explore this theme in greater depth, from the complementary perspectives of the god and his human collaborator, before attempting to sum up the conceptual structure that informs this text, above all its understanding of what happens when man meets god.

Notice, first, how the poet has handled his material on the most external level of linguistic articulation. Cekkiḻār's syntax, like that of all medieval Tamil *kāvya,* rests on relatively simple hypotaxis, intimately tied to his metrical structures; there are no pregnant silences, no truncated dialogues, no understated parataxis, such as Auerbach pointed out in the Hebrew *aqedah.*[9] Occasionally, the ornate diction wavers suggestively: at the climax of the sacrifice, past verbs give way to present-futures, as if the poet were unable to bring himself to articulate the finality of the act. Thus the mother "*gave* the child over to her husband" (*ĕṭuttuk kaṇavar kai kŏṭuttār,* 60); but they then "take him somewhere else" (i.e., not the kitchen—*veṟu kŏṇṭ' aṇaivār*) where Ciṟuttŏṇṭar "will cut off his head" (*talaiy arivār,* 61–63). The transition in tense is very striking, even moving; both parents are filled with joy, for "they will perform this difficult act" (*ariya viṉai ceyvār,* 64). Are they performing it still, in a timeless, mythic present? Is devotion, at

9. Auerbach (1957), 5–20.

base, this unfinished, always painful as well as joyful process of offering? The same alternation in tense recurs in the final moments of the story, when the reunited family "fell, arose, and praised" the visible deity *(vi̱ḻuntār, ĕḻuntār, ettiṉār)* who (continuously) "performs acts of grace" for their sake (*aruḷ purivār,* 86). The past drifts, almost unconsciously, into ongoing experience; the story is never finally told.

This slight disparity in tense may alert us to more profound imbalances. The outstanding feature of Cekkiḻār's telling, from the point of view of texture, is the incongruous mingling of semantic levels (or, more generally, of narrative content and style). A story of utmost terror unfolds in sentences replete with gentle, joyful phrases brutally juxtaposed with strategic verbs of cutting, killing, devouring. Let us take just one example, the critical verse just mentioned that describes the sacrifice (including the sudden transition to present-future tense):

iṉiya maḻalaik kiṇkiṇikkāl iraṇṭu maṭiyiṉ puṭaiy iṭukki
kaṉi vāy maintaṉ kaiy iraṇṭuṅ kaiyāṟ piṭikkak kātalaṉum
naṉi nīṭ' uvakaiy uṟukiṉṟār ĕṉṟu makiḻntu nakai cĕyyat
taṉi mā makaṉait tātaiyār karuvi kŏṇṭu talaiy arivār

She squeezed the tiny feet
onto her lap,
the anklets ringing
sweetly, as she held the two hands
of her soft-spoken child,
while he—the beloved son—
was happy, and smiled, for
"*They* are experiencing some great joy,"
he thought, and then the father
takes the knife to his one, only child
and cuts the head. (63)

The effect is clearly premeditated: a crescendo of delicious tenderness and delight—the "sweet ringing" *(iṉiya maḻalai)* of the anklet-bells, the child's soft speech (literally, "ripe mouth," *kaṉi-vāy*), the joy *(uvakai . . . makiḻntu)* that he and his parents both feel, and his eloquent title, "the beloved son" (*kātalaṉ*, from *kātal*, "desire")—builds up to the head-rhyme at the start of the final line, where we find "the one, only child" *(taṉi mā makaṉai)* as an object-accusative. The verse climaxes here, with great power, the child's status as victim confirmed and illuminated; all that remains is to conclude the line with the bitter alliteration of the father *(tātaiyār)* who cuts off the head *(talaiy arivār)*. The verse ends with this violence, that literally, iconically cuts through the loving tones that come before, thus abruptly forcing a horrific closure. And the mind protests: this conjunction of love and slaughter, so calculated in its progression, produces a sense of almost unbearable paradox; the narration as a whole is an extended, agitated oxymoron. What we see in this single verse is completely typical of the entire telling; verbs of desire, compassion, love (*pari, naya, aruḷ,* etc.) with their associated nominals and synonyms *(parivu, aruḷ, kātal, karuṇai)* almost overwhelm the listener, who is nevertheless never allowed to forget the harsh nature of the sacrificial deed embedded in this soft semantic cushion. The poetic power of the text largely depends on this disturbing, incongruous juxtaposition, with frequent, shocking transitions from one contrasting register to the other.

Such textures are always strongly suggestive. In essence, the verbal surface of this version encodes the incongruous conjunction that lies at the heart of Tamil Śaivism: Śiva's horrific qualities, his *raudra* nature that goes back to the mythology of the dread Vedic Rudra, are habitually linked in Tamil texts with his compassion *(karuṇā)*. The revelation of the former is always an enactment of the latter.[10] The terror that is truth—the truth of divinity—is made present to experience through an act of love. To this conjunction of seeming opposites we need to add a third component, which completes the semantic core of this form of Śaivism—the notion of play *(līlā, viḷaiyāṭal)*, which provides the medium through which such revelations can take place. Śiva's compassionate revelation of his terrifying mode of being is a playful act—very much akin to the poet's playful juxtaposing of sweet and brutal tones. Note that the god's play takes the specific form, in our story, of his tantalizing, rather perverse teasing of the Little Devotee (by refusing to eat the food the latter has offered him). What is this if not a game, ruthlessly pursued, beyond all reasonable limits, to the end? Yet, as we shall see, the god may have his own reasons,

10. See Shulman (1986).

no doubt closely related to the peculiar effect generated by his incongruous combination of traits. Moreover, in general, the set we have outlined—terror, mercy, play—recurs in fascinating permutations throughout the *Pĕriya Purāṇam,* usually in connection with the transformation in awareness that dynamic paradox can achieve. It is, I believe, safe to assume that some such transformation is intended here.

To sum up to this point: Cekkiḻār's version deliberately structures itself around the interplay of richly contrasting semantic and emotive elements; this contrast exists within the surface texture of the verses, with their tendency toward alarming transitions. The semantic contrast runs parallel to a thematic conjunction within Tamil Śaivism expressive of the inner constitution of the deity and of his role in the human world; horror, compassion, and playfulness are bound up in a potent amalgam that is capable of producing a change in consciousness. Something of this transformation in awareness overtakes the listener as the text is read: the stark incongruities of the texture work on the emotions, which are heightened even as "normal" logic is undermined. We may begin to suspect that a characteristic process, with certain stable features and a definite telos, lies embedded in stories of revelation like that of the Little Devotee.

4

In and Out, and the Problem of Food

To explore this process further, we turn to the major symbolic elements of our text. Let us start with a simple observation. The entire story seems to revolve around oral obsessions: Śiva is "as if" hungry, and Ciṟuttŏṇṭar spends his days feeding; he will, indeed, stop at nothing to force the Śaiva guest to eat. The sacrifice itself takes the form of a feast. Cooking, seasoning, serving, eating—this series centers the narrative structure. The Little Devotee treats his guest as god and therefore serves him in the *pūjā* mode, as the text directly states; and *pūjā* here is a transaction based on the elaborate offering of cooked food.[11] Just as in the temple the pil-

11. In the temple context, the pilgrim often brings uncooked food (such as fruit); but here the exchange takes place in the home, the recipient being a guest

grim brings food for the god to taste and to return to him as *prasāda*—a form of "grace," a benevolent gift—Ciṟuttŏṇṭar cooks and offers up his son, only to receive him back in a similar demonstration of the god's merciful connection. The *pūjā* paradigm is sensual, transactional, transformative, and primarily oral. Internalization, in this context, means the literal consumption of the devotee's gift.

Internalization of this sort, by the divine guest, is precisely Ciṟuttŏṇṭar's goal. The always critical boundary between inner and outer is meant to be crossed. We should notice, however, that such boundary-crossings are a *general* concern in our story, on various levels, including the fundamental depiction of movement through space. Stated abstractly, this is a story of continuous movement inwards toward a point of final implosion, when a reversal suddenly takes place. Śiva leaves his heaven—mythic space identified in Tamil as a form of *puṟam,* the "outside" domain—to come down to a Tamil village, where he enters a home; the drama then culminates in the innermost space *(akam)* of that home, the kitchen and dining area.[12] Ciṟuttŏṇṭar's consistent effort is to draw his guest into this intimate family space. This, then, is a narrative of domestic "innerness" invaded by, or opened toward, a force from the mythic outside. Only in the final moments of the narrative is the boundary crossed in the opposite direction: Ciṟuttŏṇṭar and his wife emerge from their house to call their son; Ciṟuttŏṇṭar reenters the home only to find that his guest, and the prepared curries, have disappeared; he races back outside in time to see the god in his externalized epiphany. So, inside we have the cannibalistic horror, in a setting of domestic intimacy and violence; outside, there is the revelation and the melting/merging of the devotees into their god. The story is telling us something about the meaning of innerness, the inner space, the home—that violence and intimacy may go together, for example, may even be interde-

who is prepared to receive cooked food from his hosts—thereby also, on some level, acknowledging their higher position. We pursue this theme of relative hierarchy between guest and host, god and devotee, below.

12. On *akam* and *puṟam* as fundamental cultural categories in South India, see Ramanujan (1986). Though the child is apparently not killed in the kitchen, the climactic scene is still located in the dining area inside the house.

pendent; or that the domestic and the everyday contain some kernel of potential horror. Ciruttŏṇṭar is a prototypical householder who, as the disguised ascetic derisively tells him, eats every day, never missing a meal. Although the life of the home is certainly seen in the Tamil country as a major arena of the sacred,[13] it is also—partly by this very identification—a site of potential conflict and aggression.

Here, however, the aggressive impulse is *initiated* by the divine force from outside, then carried out by the father (and mother) within the family setting. This progression is important; we can, I think, be more precise both about the actual workings and the potential meanings of this movement across the boundary. Keeping in mind the persistent focus on internalization, in the two forms we have mentioned—physical consumption of the offering, and absorption into the inner realm of the home—we need to explore in some detail the motivations of both major actors in this drama, the god and his servant/devotee. Why do they join forces in this obsessive matter of food and feeding? We begin with Śiva and his peculiar hunger.

5

On Eating

Recall the rationale Cekkiḻār offers for Śiva's descent to Tiruccĕṅkāṭṭaṅkuṭi: he wants to savor the love whose essence is truth. The verb, *nukar,* describes a range of sensual experiences—savoring, tasting, enjoying, knowing in or through the body.[14] It is very striking that the god is driven in this direction, as if he were unable or unwilling to leave love, *aṉpu*—his devotee's love, which Śiva clearly needs—in some nonmaterialized, purely internal form. There is, then, a countervailing movement on the level of the divinity: not only does he come from the outer divine sphere to the inner world of the human home, but he seems also to enact a movement from a more abstract and internal mode of being to an externalized, sensuous one. Love, to be real, cannot be rele-

13. See Hart (1979).

14. In PP 1209, for instance, the gods come down to "taste" or "consume" their portions of the Brahmins' sacrifices at Ceyñalūr (*aviy uṇavin̲ pāka' nukara*).

gated to ethereal imaginings, or even to a divine form of all-encompassing knowledge; it has to be tasted, confronted, lived out through sensory and emotional experience in the outer world. This is the inherent teleology of emotion in a Tamil universe, and our story follows it through to the end. The connection between god and human beings is a passionate one; contrary to the ideology of Yoga, which attacks, suppresses, and seeks to transcend emotion and sensory cognition, Tamil *bhakti* uses them as primary means of metaphysical accomplishment. Any true linkage between the deity and his followers has to take into account this dimension of sensual perception, which the god also actively seeks. Tasting or savoring are not "mere" metaphors for this process of establishing connection but, rather, literal concretizations of its essential dynamics. One loves in a volatile, complicated, partly destructive, sometimes bewildering, but always tangible, sensate mode.

Evidently, this is true of the deity no less than of us; he, too, is subject to passion, which is defined as hunger. We could formulate the issue slightly differently, as an assertion—actually an intuition, indeed one of the most fundamental of Tamil intuitive notions about the world—that the real always has a taste; that is, that embodied sensual experience can subsume the unrealized potentialities and distances within the unembodied deity. Such a formulation, that has emerged out of the text's own attempt to explain this problematic story, may well surprise us, accustomed as we are to the more common Vedāntic belief that the more subtle, abstract, and inner always encompass and subsume the gross, concrete, and external. Still, there is, it seems, a way in which this conventional hierarchy can be inverted, thus privileging the drive toward the manifest exterior, the visible, audible, tastable form. We need only think again of the Tamil temple, with its sensually enlivened rituals of *pūjā,* to begin to recognize the forcefulness of Cekkiḻār's stand.[15]

This is one sense in which we can understand Śiva's hunger. Indeed, so basic is this perception that one is tempted to add the

15. On the tensions between sensual and emotional openness and the Yogic strand in Tamil *bhakti,* see Hardy (1983). Hardy sees the limitations inherent in sensory experience of the absolute as a source for the elaborate theology of *viraha,*

category of hunger—*paci* in Tamil—to the list of three existential categories recognized by the Śaiva Siddhāntins in their philosophical summation of Tamil devotionalism (from a slightly later period than Cekkiḻār). Each of these terms also begins with the phoneme "p": first *pati,* the Lord; then *paśu,* literally "the beast" (the same term used by Śiva in demanding a sacrifice from Ciṟuttŏṇṭar), i.e., the embodied spirit or being; finally *pāśa,* the state of bondage characterizing existence in the world. These categories, which have no end and no beginning, are felt to exhaust creation; they are also inherently asymmetrical, God being endowed with ontic superiority vis-à-vis the other two. If, however, we add *paci* to this set, we will have a counterpart on the divine level to *pāśa,* the bondage afflicting the human level. God hungers for human love—for the embodied *paśu*—experienced in external ways. The Śaiva Siddhāntins would, of course, object to this impertinence; to these philosophers, God is pure, free, entirely independent of any need. But to the Tamil storytellers and poets from an earlier time in the evolution of the Śaiva tradition, such a definition of the deity misses the most essential point. The god of Ciṟuttŏṇṭar and Cekkiḻār needs and seeks to live out an intense, animating desire; his very being appears to generate a violent hunger that drives him continuously toward this world.

But there is another meaning to the hunger. After all, we can still ask why the "savoring" Śiva seeks must take this particularly gruesome form. Would not the revelation granted at the end have served to call forth the same emotion even earlier, without the terror and pain of the sacrifice? Apparently not—the revelation proceeds directly, and perhaps necessarily, out of this sacrifice. We have to remember that Hindu notions of divinity frequently include the aspect of the all-devouring Absolute. It is, as the Bhairava ascetic correctly informs Ciṟuttŏṇṭar, quite impossible to satisfy this hunger. The Whole ultimately consumes the beings it has created: Arjuna sees this truth in the Viśvarūpa form of Kṛṣṇa, whose gaping mouths chew and swallow endless streams of living

separation and its consequent mood of longing, in Tamil devotional texts. Note, however, that the story of Ciṟuttŏṇṭar ends with a total transcendence of *viraha;* the devotees melt into the god. It would appear that the process of revelation described here offers a way out of the unending labyrinth of separation.

creatures.[16] Mārkaṇḍeya, the long-lived sage, keeps falling out of, and then back into, the mouth of God; all the worlds, he learns, exist tenuously inside the deity as little more than a gastric illusion, whose substance is death or digestion.[17] The Śiva of our tale is but another in this ghastly series, even if his destructive energy is directed only at a single chosen victim.

Hence the overriding need for sacrifice: this is one form of the devotee's surrender, a meeting and connection that incorporate the destructiveness inherent to divinity. There is no way past this terror except by going through it, to the end. Only Death—Śiva as Kāla—can be the end of death (Kālāntaka, another prominent title for this god).[18] The sacrifice must therefore be complete, and include even the child's head. Here Cekkiḻār resumes a classical theme: Vedic sacrificial texts often speak of the "head of the sacrifice," the final element that also serves as remnant, hence the seed of future sacrifices. To achieve *(sam-āp)* the ritual, one must offer the head.[19] Ciṟuttŏṇṭar nearly fails in this respect—it is only the maidservant, Cantaṉattār, who saves him, and renders the offering whole. Note, too, how the sacrifice allows for no "interiorization" in the older, Vedic sense—that is, no symbolic rearticulation, and above all no form of substitution or surrogate victim, both central elements in the mature Vedic cult.[20] Here the ritual has to be literally carried through, with all its attendant violence, upon the prescribed victim, who can never be redundant or subject to exchange. This, too, fits the vision of a hungry, demanding, unrelenting god.

It is not an easy vision. For all the talk of joyful offering—an incongruous joy, as we have seen—the Tamil literary tradition is hardly at peace with the god's demand. Another Chola-period text, the *Tillai ulā,* referring to the story, actually calls this request for the child victim an "evil act" *(pātakam);* it also speaks of the god's great hunger *(pĕrum paci),* which required the meat of the head, and of his eyes which, strangely, were not ashamed to see

16. *Bhagavadgītā* 11.

17. *MBh* 3.186; Doniger [O'Flaherty] (1980).

18. See Shulman (1983); *Tevāram* of Cuntaramūrtti 540–49; Sivaraman (1973), 50.

19. See Heesterman (1967).

20. Heesterman (1962); Doniger and Smith (1989).

the dreadful curries prepared for him *(kūcāta kaṇṇum)*.[21] These are ironic statements, yet they surely express something of the natural aversion the story arouses. Even if the revelation of the god's all-consuming nature is, ultimately, a form of mercy, the actual sacrifice—especially in this case of a beloved and innocent child—remains imbued with horror. At the very least, we must recognize Śiva's willingness to instigate and witness this killing. Its meaning within the wider process as a whole, including the eventual revival of the victim, is still to be explored; for now, let us point again to the two forces motivating the god—his desired devolution outward, toward the human world in its sensate and emotional intensity; and his very real, always active hunger, that derives logically from the destructive relation of the Absolute to his creatures.

6

On Feeding

As it happens, this divine hunger coincides all too perfectly with the human needs of the devotee. The core of the story is, indeed, structured around this coincidence: *bhakti* metaphysics interlock with a medieval South Indian psychology and theory of the emotions. If Śiva wants to eat, his servant longs to feed him. In effect, the two parties collude in what can almost be considered a crime (as the passage just quoted, from the *Tillai ulā,* confirms). We have, then, to consider Ciṟuttŏṇṭar's side of this equation.

There are, no doubt, ancient roots to the Little Devotee's compulsion. Much earlier Śaiva texts recommend feeding any guest—always seen as a form of the god—as a means of freeing the host from evil; the guest transfers to himself, and absorbs, the host's burden of evil *karma* in the course of devouring the latter's food.[22] But Ciṟuttŏṇṭar goes much farther than this theory would demand, and his motivation appears to be more ambiguous and complex. On the one hand, he, too, is drawn to externalize and concretize the bond of love; in this context, food *is* love—or perhaps it would be more precise to say that eating, on the part of the Śaiva guest, is the necessary tangible sign that the love-relation is

21. *Tillai ulā* 197ff., cited in Dorai Rangaswamy (1959), 1012.
22. See Doniger [O'Flaherty] (1973), 182–84.

active, effective, and real. The guest's consumption of food marks the acceptance and final internalization of the devotee's gift. On the other hand, we should not be misled by Ciṟuttŏṇṭar's title, and by the outwardly humble stance that it implies, into assuming that there is no dynamic of power exchanges taking place. Quite the contrary: in south India, as elsewhere, the giver of love enjoys a meaningful advantage over the recipient.[23] This is particularly true of the *bhakti* relationship, where the devotee, by offering love, seeks and achieves a form of superiority over the god he serves. *Bhagavāṉilum mempaṭṭavar bhāgavatar,* states the Tamil proverb: the devotee is greater even than his god. In the context of worship, the loving devotee's advantage translates into conditions of heightened autonomy; he has the upper hand, and can claim to control the interaction by purely emotional means. He can blackmail the god, turn his own helplessness to advantage, set the tone of the exchanges. Love, *aṉpu,* is both a goal and a means: Ciṟuttŏṇṭar, as the text tells us, "conquers through love" (*aṉpiṉ vĕṉṟa tŏṇṭar,* 86). Whom has he conquered if not the god, his tantalizing partner and tormentor? We begin to see why Ciṟuttŏṇṭar's frustration at not being able to feed his guest is far greater, far more compelling, than even the horror of sacrificing his son.

And there is still more to this need. *Pūjā,* too, as we have said, revolves around offerings of food. This move across the inner/outer border has both ontic and psychological meaning; it speaks to the issue of the god's position, on both sides of the boundary, and to the human anxiety lest the deity disappear. The Tamil devotee knows the god as part of himself, perhaps even the deepest, truest part; the experience repeatedly described by the poets is one of sudden revelation-through-possession, when the god miraculously enters into and takes control of the human self.[24] But this same god, this same divine part of the self, then has the unhappy habit of vanishing, of denying access; the devotee, whose personality has been disrupted by the meeting, is given over to an unending search for the absent lover, embedded somewhere within him.

23. Trawick [Egnor] (1980).

24. E.g., *Tiruvāymŏḻi* of Nammāḻvār, 10.7.1–2; *Tiruvācakam* of Māṇikkavācakar, *tiruccatakam* 3.2: "As I was lying, caught in deeds, you entered me and remained inside . . ." And see Hudson (1989).

But Śiva is *not only* inside; he can also be found in the world, in the home or temple, in the Tamil village. There, too, of course, his presence tends to be revealed by capricious absence—as when the Little Devotee rushes back with his son into the dining room, only to find that his guest has gone. Indeed, this type of contact, informed by the recognition of absence, constitutes a major paradigm—hence the compulsive need to reestablish the divine presence, to capture the divinity and hold him in place, at least for a fleeting moment. *Pūjā,* including above all the transfer of food, is one powerful means of accomplishing this goal.

Eating, being eaten—these are the essential forms of contact. We take the other into ourselves, and are ourselves consumed. From the devotee's standpoint, in order for the process to be complete, inner substance—the food that, in this case, is the servant's own son—has to cross the boundary and be absorbed within the god, in his guise as outsider. His eating would guarantee his presence, his reality, his acceptance of the devotee's gift of self. The process is interactional, fueled both by the god's hunger and by the human longing for incorporation within the elusive deity. But this process is also powerfully transformative: in effect, at the moment of internalization, as outer passes inward, both identities mingle and expand. The concrete transition accomplished in the world of deeds—first the importunate demands, then sacrificial violence, serving and (almost) eating—signals and confirms a transition within the self. Am I, at bottom, Śiva? Is he inside me or not? How can I know? Does this "I," this residual, refractory ego, still exist after having touched the god? Can I divest myself of this "I" to the point where only "he" is left? In the realistic universe of Tamil *bhakti,* these questions can only be tested—one hesitates to say resolved—by enacting a movement through the outer domain, from inner, fractured self toward the embodied divinity and back again. The movement changes both parties to the process in line with their complementary needs.

In effect, one part of the self—that connected with love for an only son, in the context of the home and its demands on identity—is being offered up to another, less accessible and familiar part, identified with the peculiar innerness that is god. The goal is to make this latter part present, in a more stable way, to conscious experience, with the accompanying transformative effects upon awareness, perception, and bodily sensation. It nevertheless remains crucial to the Tamil Śaiva understanding of the world that this process of achieving connection is not limited to an internal psychic space: the god is real, capable (and desirous) of externalization, at home in both "outer" *(puṟam)* and "inner" *(akam)* modes. Or, stated differently: the inner form of being that is sought by the devotee can be reached only by the total, lived-through experience of real sacrifice, with its inherent features of violent negation—the offering up of life—and unmediated, raw emotion. Giving, in the real world, connects, via loss and paradox, with a living truth that is hidden inside.

Wanting to feed, desperately needing to feed, thus corresponds to a certain mode of innerness, a mode that also entails a vital yearning to be eaten oneself—probably by a hungry part of one's own fractured self. The god/guest must somehow be forced to eat in the interests of allaying the anxiety and existential confusion that are rife within the devotee/host. In this sense, Ciṟuttŏṇṭar seems to function as one type of mother, while the god acts, all too appropriately, like a fractious child, reluctant to swallow what is being offered to him (as the result of his own initial request).[25] Indeed, Ciṟuttŏṇṭar's maternal guise is very much in evidence from the start, even before the Bhairava ascetic comes to the village; it is precisely by compulsive feeding that this devotee wins his title and his fame, which eventually compel Śiva to assume *his* disturbing role.

Alongside this fanatic male "mother" we also observe the child-victim's *real* mother, Vĕṇkāṭṭunaṅkai, who goes along with her husband's extreme demands and also responds, so we are told, with the same excess of incongruous joy. Let us take a moment to scrutinize her side of the interaction. In our text, the mother never initiates a major development; she even seems momentarily to hesitate when her husband first presents her with the sacrificial scenario; but she is, from that point on, entirely complicit in the deed,

25. I wish to thank Wendy Doniger for this observation. South Indian *bhakti* texts often play with the image of the devotee as mother to the deity, as when the poet imagines himself as Devakī or Yaśodā, mothers to the infant Kṛṣṇa; the devotee thus relates to his god in the mode of *vātsalya,* the cow's tender emotion toward its calf. In the present instance of Ciṟuttŏṇṭar, Tamil Śaivism characteristically introduces an ironic and partly antagonistic twist to this pattern.

and deeply implicated in the totalistic emotional stance that it requires. There are, however, two further aspects of her experience that the Tamil text makes clear: first, she is particularly capable of the transformative inner movement of softening and opening that the entire process is meant to foster; something in her nature seems to allow her to unfold and blossom, "like a bud," at the very height of the terror and violence in which she so actively participates. Second, it is Vĕṇkāṭṭunaṅkai who, far more than her husband, seems open to the paradoxical moment of calling out to the slaughtered child; knowing he is dead, she nevertheless poignantly and lyrically summons him to return, and it is thus first to her embrace that the boy naturally runs. This mother might be said to live out the paradoxical sequence—the violence of love and surrender, an inner affirmation in the context of ultimate loss, an openness to the surrealistic restoration of the victim out of faith in his continued emotional presence in awareness—even more directly and fully than does her frenzied husband, who retains residual elements of doubt and despair. In short, the harshly maternal male, intent on feeding, is paired with a no less determined wife and mother who yet represents the whole promise implicit in the process the two must undergo. Not surprisingly, perhaps, as will be seen in the next chapter, this feminine role undergoes significant expansion in the later South Indian versions of our story.

We can now see why the notion of testing or trial in the Abrahamic sense is so foreign to the Tamil version of this story. The entire process has a different logic. This is not, or not yet, a story of God's testing the loyalty and worthiness of a man, but rather a drama of intimacy played out in heart and home. It explores with great clarity the components and dynamics of love for, and by, a god, and the nature of the meeting between this god and his devotees. A ravenous, in some sense murderous god is compelled to taste human love, in a violent and sensual demonstration of the bond that links him to his servants; for his part, the devotee is also hungry, even desperate, for the autonomy and triumph that come with successfully force-feeding the object of his devotion—and for the form of stable presence, inside and out, that could ensue from this act. Contrasting motivations push toward the sacrifice, which, as usual, fastens on the most vulnerable figure as victim; this sacrifice establishes the conditions for real contact between the main figures and for the mutual transformation consequent upon their meeting. Let us try now, in concluding this chapter, to formulate more carefully, and more abstractly, the basic sequence.

7

On Transformation

Here, again, are the major stages: the god assumes a disguise and descends to earth; he demands the terrible offering (the first meeting, a hidden revelation, with the god present and visible, speaking human language to punning yet literal effect); the sacrifice is carried out, and all parties enter the surreal boundary zone of potential transformation; inside this boundary, the god plays with his devotee, frustrating and tormenting him, up to the moment when reason is finally superseded and a reversal can take place; the reversal leads to an overt revelation, that depends on the god's absence from the inner space of the home, and that proceeds in total silence. Ciṟuttŏṇṭar and his family, so we are told, have been totally transformed; they will never be separate from the god again. Śiva, too, it is safe to infer, has had his taste of human love.

This process has a general applicability to the stories of Tamil Śaivism, although many variations exist. Its basic elements—disguise on the part of the god; a playful revelation that leads to violence, ultimately reversed in the course of a transition to a new form of being or awareness; and a final epiphany on this new level, which entails an absence on the former one—are stable features of both hagiographical and Tamil purāṇic texts. Śiva almost never simply shows himself, "as he is" (if such a phrase has any meaning), without undergoing the playful movement of disguise; and there seems to be no other way to achieve the existential transformation that, if I am right, is the final object of this kind of tale. A zigzag pattern of disguise, displacement, and belated recognition seems to be the shortest, or at any rate the most dependable, route. Part of this pattern is the sacrificial action, which may well also, in some sense, be displaced.

Let us ask ourselves once more: is this sacrifice really necessary? Why must it take this particularly gruesome, filicidal form? We might speculate that the initial violent impulse transpires elsewhere, within the divine being with his consuming desire; and that this violence to the divine self is transferred, in the general outward vector that marks Śiva's descent, to the devotee who is asked to offer up what he most loves. In this case, the notion of empathetic identification, which we saw in the story of Maṉunīticoḻaṉ, is effectively reversed, and it is the devotee who takes on himself the burden of the god's need and pain.[26] In any case, the aggression that the parents direct against their son is not really proper to that intrafamily axis; rather, it reflects the intricate relations between Ciṟuttŏṇṭar and the deity. As we have seen, intimacy is bound up with violence in these Śaiva stories. Margaret Trawick, in a masterful description of love in a Tamil home, speaks of "sequential contrast" as one important component of the love relation: "opposites were shown to depend upon one another and to generate one another";[27] angry rejection easily issues into welcoming acceptance, even temporary fusion. Such pendulum swings have a different dynamic from the zigzag movement we have mentioned, but the result is similar: love, even in its "positive" aspect of caring and giving, includes the various "negative" powers of aggression.

Indeed, it is these "negative" powers that enable the longed-for transformation. Without them, the border would never be crossed. However tortuous the path, however indirect and rich in displacements, the meeting of Śiva and Ciṟuttŏṇṭar succeeds in merging two distinct levels of being. It is a meeting that transpires inside, in the home, and in the devotee's awareness; not by chance, it fastens on the son, the primary embodiment of this inner domain. From ancient times, the young child has epitomized for Tamil poets the sense and purpose of the loving family, at home in the inner space *(akam)* where emotion counts most of all:

> Even when a man has earned much
> of whatever can be earned,
> shared it with many,
> even when he is master of great estates,
>
> if he does not have
> children

26. This pattern is familiar from much earlier Indian texts, for example, the myths of Indra's brahminicide, divided among various earthly and human carriers: see Doniger [O'Flaherty] (1976), 146–60, 168–73.

27. Trawick (1990), p. 250.

who patter on their little feet,
stretch tiny hands,
scatter, touch,
grub with mouths
and grab with fingers,
smear rice and ghee
all over their bodies,
and overcome reason with love,

all his days
have come to nothing.[28]

Thus the Caṅkam poet Pāṇṭiyaṉ Aṟivuṭai Nampi, in a verse that seems almost to set the stage for Cekkiḻār's much later tale of sacrifice: notice the central image of eating, and the theme of "overcoming reason with love" (*aṟivai iṉpattāṉ mayakkum putalvar,* as the medieval commentator states). Only Cekkiḻār goes a step farther, in line with the process of radical transformation that he is pursuing: the person whose life would, in the medieval Śaiva context, "come to nothing" is the one who, blessed with a child whom he adores, fails to offer him, overcoming reason, if and when the god demands.

28. *Puṟanāṉūṟu* 188, translation by A. K. Ramanujan (1985), 160.

3

Ciruttŏṇṭar/Siriyāla in the Telugu Tradition

1

The story of the Little Devotee is not an easy one—not for us, and not for the South Indian Śaiva tradition. Just how problematic it was felt to be becomes clear as we move northwards from the Tamil country, with its primary version of the tale, to Andhra and the various retellings in Telugu, Tamil's sister-language. The Telugu versions we will examine radically rework the story as it exists in Tamil (and we may safely assume that some Tamil version close to that of Cekkiḻār, if not the *Pĕriya Purāṇam* text itself, was familiar to the Śaiva poets of medieval Andhra). We will see how an internal critique of the story emerges in these Telugu sources, and how they transform the contours of the text in highly determined, programmatic ways. At the same time, we will be interested in the distinct social and cultural contexts that generated these changes, and in the specific values they reflect.

We begin with a relatively short version from the Telugu Vīraśaiva work, *Basavapurāṇamu,* by the thirteenth-century poet Pālkuriki Somanātha. This poet, composing largely in the popular *dvipada* meter, inherited the whole corpus of Tamil Śaiva hagiography, much of which he (or his tradition) reworked in innovative

This chapter largely represents the joint work of David Shulman and Velcheru Narayana Rao.

ways; he also recontextualized these stories by framing them within the even more melodramatic narratives of the Vīraśaiva heroes. As we shall see in the case of Ciṟuttŏṇṭar, this narrative framing is also a very powerful form of commentary and reflection. Deccani Vīraśaivism inhabits a wholly different universe from that of Cekkiḻār and his Tamil Śaiva predecessors; within this new setting, our story takes on different meanings, different textures, unexpected themes.

What can we say, in brief, about this Vīraśaiva universe? It is, to begin with, iconoclastic, rebellious, angry, with a pronounced fondness for violent tones. Its enemy is the *sthāvara*—anything fixed, immobile, fully formed, burdened with the authority of text, priest, or institution. By the same token, its ideal is the *jaṅgama*—the ever moving, the dynamic, fluid and unstable.[1] Above all, spontaneous, passionate feeling—the passion of ultimate commitment—motivates the Vīrásaiva poets and saints. They are, themselves, *jaṅgamas,* wandering devotees, in love with Śiva conceived in generally monistic terms. The panoply of iconic images and temples, so prominent in Tamil *bhakti* religion, has been rejected with scorn, and the *jaṅgamas* carry only the aniconic *liṅga* as a sign of their god.

Historically, the "sect" as we know it goes back to Basava, mystic poet and antinomian politician in twelfth-century Kalyan, in the Western Deccan (although the Vīraśaiva tradition itself speaks of a much more ancient chain of teaching); its foundation texts are the Kannada *vacanas* of Basava, Mahādeviyakka, Allamaprabhu, and many others.[2] By the early thirteenth century, the movement had spread east into Andhra and inspired a creative outburst in Telugu: Somanātha's *Basavapurāṇamu* is the oldest surviving hagiography of Basava, and one of the oldest and most complete accounts of the Vīraśaivas' formative period in general.[3] We see in it the traces of fierce ideological (and probably also physical) struggles—with the *bhavis,* i.e., the "worldly" who rejected the absolute commitment to Śiva; with the Jains, a constant menace outside the Hindu fold; above all, perhaps, with the Brahmins,

1. See Ramanujan (1973); Narayana Rao (1990).
2. Ibid.; see also Nandimath (1942).
3. On the spread and institutionalization of Vīraśaivism in Andhra, see Shulman (1992b).

within it. Though Basava was himself a Brahmin, he brazenly attacked the ordered universe of Brahmin social and ritual theory; bounded castes, a hierarchized social ontology, the hallowed scheme of ritualized progression through life's fixed stages *(varṇāśramadharma)*—all this gave way before a militant, egalitarian devotionalism imbued with values from the subversive Upaniṣadic and yogic streams. It is an impatient movement, in love with an exclusive and absolutized truth, and prepared to fight for it; it is not by chance that its exemplary figures are classed as *vīras*, "heroes." It is also fitting that it takes the wild, unruly, "heretical" Śiva as its image of God.

Vīraśaivism also differs from Tamil Śaivism in its social composition. This is a matter of central importance to our understanding of the *Basavapurāṇamu*. If Cekkiḻār and the *Pĕriya Purāṇam* represent a "right-hand" vision of the world, generated mostly from high non-Brahmin castes like the Veḷāḷas, the *Basavapurāṇamu* shows us the world as perceived by "left-hand" groups such as merchants and artisans—castes not directly tied down to agriculture and the land. The values associated with the "left" tend to be more universalistic, radical, perhaps subversive, and closer to internalized self-sacrifice than to objectified blood-sacrifice (such as we find in the majority of the *Pĕriya Purāṇam* stories).[4] There is a horror of compromise and paradox, a drive toward absolutization, hence toward straightening out the zigzag patterns so characteristic of the Tamil Śaiva universe. God is present—in the palm of the hand, in the *liṅga* worn around the neck, in the inner being of the devotee—and this familiar, continuous presence makes existential demands of an ultimate character on the person. They can in no way be evaded: any hesitation, to say nothing of negation, entails an ultimate price. Indeed, as we will see, Śiva himself is forced reluctantly to absorb this existential commitment to absolute principles.

In striking contrast to the *Pĕriya Purāṇam*, the *Basavapurāṇamu* stories focus exclusively (with the exception of borrowed Tamil tales) on exemplary figures drawn from the mobile left-hand groups. It is thus not surprising that our hero, Ciṟuttŏṇṭar—

4. Ibid.; Narayana Rao (1986).

known here as Siriyāla[5] or Ciṟuttŏṇḍa Nambi—now belongs to a merchant (vaiśya) caste and lives not in a Tamil village but in the more properly left-hand environment of a city, Kāñcipuram:

Every day Siriyāla, keeping to a vow he had made, would feed five jaṅgamas whatever they wished.[6] Seeking to test the depths of his devotion (siriyālu bhaktilŏt' arayāgā talāci), Śiva went there in the guise of an ascetic. Siriyāla welcomed him: "Please come at once to help me keep my vow."

The ascetic, as if he were a compassionate person (sadayūḍa polĕ) showering mercy on Siriyāla, made a strange request for human flesh (naramāṃsamu).

"You know everything," said Siriyāla; "there is a wonderful son in my house, who is endowed with all good qualities—so what need is there for me to go and ask for human flesh at a neighbor's house?" And he rushed home to tell his wife, Sangaḷavva.[7]

"Don't worry," she said, and went to fetch her son from school; she told him this day was a festival for them, and made him beautiful for the sacrifice (vadhyaśṛṅgārambu sesi). Then the father and mother, eager for release, as if playing a game (līla), their hearts full (niṇḍāru manamuna), killed the boy, cut up his body, and prepared the various curries.

They called the god, washed his feet and drank the water; worshiping him, they served the food. He looked carefully over the various dishes and said, "There is no head-meat here. You have hidden it in order to preserve your love for your son. This isn't right, and won't fulfill the vow. The sacred texts tell us that the head is the chief limb of the body: this statement has not yet been fulfilled."

"We were afraid the food would be polluted by hair," said the

5. No doubt a Telugu form of Cīrāḷaṉ, the name of Ciṟuttŏṇṭar's son in the Tamil tradition!

6. In keeping with the embedded nature of the story in the BP, where it is presented as having taken place prior to the tale of Nimmavva which provides its context, I adopt the past tense for this summary.

7. = Tiruvĕṇkāṭṭunaṅkai; the BP also refers to her as Tiruvĕṅgāṇinaṅga, a derivative of the Tamil name. Other Telugu versions call her Tiruvĕṅganāñci (again derived from the Tamil); see below.

The moment of sacrifice. Lepakshi, Andhra Pradesh. Photo: courtesy Yigal Bronner.

two parents; "but Candanaṅga (the maidservant) will prepare it at once."

When Candanaṅga brought this last curry, the guest was pleased: "No one can compare to you as givers of food. Now, as is only proper for this gift, you must sit beside me and eat—otherwise, I am going away."

The merchant was confused and afraid *(bhayabhrantī bŏndi),* but he looked at his wife and said, "Why do you hesitate? Come!" They sat down beside their guest. He said: "When serving a guest, good people have their sons eat with them. I don't see your son, Siriyāla. How can someone like me eat in a house without a son? There is a Sanskrit saying, 'A person without a son has no path' *(aputrasya gatir nāsti)*—and ascetics certainly wouldn't eat in a home of someone without a path. If you have a son, call him. If you do not, I can't accept this food."

Siriyāla, his whole body shaking, bowed and said: "I do have a son; he is probably studying or playing somewhere. Soon he will come to receive your blessing. But for now, please protect us by eating the food—it is getting cold."

Now the guest turned to the woman. "Won't you do as I have asked? Are there children who won't come when their mother calls? Stand facing the four directions in turn, raise your voice, and call him so that we, too, can hear."

"Why argue?" she thought. She went out, faced east, and began to call: "Come, my son, who destroys the *karma* amassed in former births. Come, my child, who can conquer the god of death himself. Come: you do away with the sadness of future births and deaths. Come: you are dear to the heart of the best of yogis, who rules the north [Śiva]. . . . [8] Won't you come, my Sīrāla? The sun is setting in the west. Come, my dear, to take this sacred food *(prasādambu)* in the presence of this companion to the lord of wealth, to make it sweet to his taste."

And, as all three worlds looked on, while even the gods felt doubt (that this was really happening), the child came running, his anklets ringing, into his mother's arms. Then Śiva, the god of gods, revealed himself, and the family fell at his feet, as if they had just

8. For a complete translation of this beautiful passage, see Narayana Rao (1990), 146–47.

The women prepare the boy's head to serve to the god. Lepakshi, Andhra Pradesh. Photo: courtesy Yigal Bronner.

The boy's head (detail of figure 7). Lepakshi, Andhra Pradesh. Photo: courtesy Yigal Bronner.

awoken from a dream. The god took Candanaṅga and her loved ones, the parents and child, and all the seven neighborhoods of Kāñci back with him to Kailāsa in golden chariots.[9]

Thus the now familiar story, told with economy and directness in rapidly flowing *dvipada* verse. Seen alone, and without entering into issues of style and texture at this point, this version makes only a few important changes. The Little Devotee has a new name, Siriyāla, and, as already noted, a different social identity; he lives in the great city of Kāñci; his vow is to feed five Śaiva *jaṅgamas* every day. More striking in the light of our discussion of Cekkiḻār is the motivation ascribed to Śiva: this time, as in the Biblical *aqedah,* the story is a trial; the god wishes to examine the depths of Siriyāla's *bhakti.* As we shall see, this motif is by no means as simple as it might seem, and the notion of depth is certainly appropriate. The initial conversation between Śiva and Siriyāla is short and to the point, without the punning obliquity of the Tamil version; the god asks simply for human flesh, not specifying the age or nature of the victim, and it is Siriyāla who *volunteers* his son for this sacrifice. This is a major departure from the *Pĕriya Purāṇam;* its effect is to transfer at least part of the violent impulse from the deity to his shockingly eager devotee. The child's awareness plays no part whatsoever in the tale; he is swiftly killed by the two parents, who are said to be as if absorbed in a game *(līlā).* Here, too, a theme focused earlier on the god has been moved to his human servant; one senses already a certain shift in the balance of forces at work in the story.

The conversation in the dining room takes on a somewhat ironic tone: the god sardonically accuses the parents of keeping the boy's head as a memento; and his demand that Siriyāla call his son is couched in a seemingly ingenuous, but actually rather brutal form. Recall that here, in contrast with the Tamil version, the guest is assumed by Siriyāla to be perfectly aware of the victim's identity from the start. The shaken father still plays along, begging the god to go ahead and eat; he *does* have a son, he lies, promising that the boy will turn up "later." But the clear climax of the story—a poetic tour de force resonant with tenderness and a love

9. *BP* 4, 115–18.

that overpowers death—is the mother's call to her child. Everything in the text strives toward this point of tension and transcendence. Elegant Sanskrit compounds mix with the intimate Telugu imperatives (*rāvĕ, rāvayya*—"Come!"), repeated in an intoxicating crescendo which seems to sweep reality before it; in the mother's heart, the child is alive and must respond; the cognitive dissonance in the mind of the reader, who can hardly forget that the child is dead, quickly dissolves in the flooding, magical vocatives. After this, the boy's reappearance is almost anticlimactic, as is the family's subsequent removal to Śiva's world.

We could address these changes, taken together—they do point toward a certain direction of transformation—but the more far-reaching innovations are still to come. For the story of Siriyāla forms part of another, far more extreme story in the *Basavapurāṇamu*—that of Nimmavva (which has a sequel relating to another devotee, Halāyudha). Before pursuing our analysis, let us see how this expanded frame works upon our story.

2

Nimmavva

The linkage has to do with Siriyāla's pride: once translated to heaven in the way we have seen, he happily announces to Śiva that no other devotee has ever equaled his, Siriyāla's, amazing deed. This boast, a kind of mad delusion *(krŏvvu),* prompts an immediate response. Śiva takes Siriyāla by the hand, and the two descend again to earth, to the home of the woman Nimmavva.

Although she is not expecting guests, Nimmavva at once brings them into her house, washes their feet, and sends them to sleep while she prepares their meal. When she leaves for a moment to fetch water, her young son comes home hungry and finds the newly baked cakes *(būrĕ);* he takes a bite out of one. His mother, returning, immediately knows. "You dog!" she cries and—since he has nibbled at the food that was meant for Śiva (i.e., the sleeping guests)—she takes a piece of firewood and smashes the boy's skull. Without even an ant's measure of attachment to her son, she throws the body on a dunghill and covers it with trash. Then she returns to the kitchen. At this, Śiva—who has only pretended to be asleep—nudges Siriyāla, and the latter, amazed, nods his head.

Finally, the meal is ready; the two guests are invited to be served. Now Śiva—rather like a vaudeville magician about to perform a well-tried, favorite trick that has always worked before—turns to Nimmavva and says, "Lady, just a minute ago there was a young boy here, who seemed to be very hungry. He must be your son. Where has he gone? Why are you serving us without feeding him? It isn't right to eat when there are hungry children around. You seem to have no compassion in your heart. Call your son quickly."

And this time the trick fails. Here is Nimmavva's reply (in the precise translation of Velcheru Narayana Rao):

"Do you think you can get by with this just because I am a woman? I know your magic. And I am not stupid, Black Neck. Why do you keep trying to tell me stories? Do you mistake me for Siriyāla? You cannot get away without eating this food. Do you think that I am ignorant and that I will be deluded by you? Do you think that I am tied to my child? Now that I have killed my son, I am not going to call him back again. Kāma Killer, I do not want anything to do with the Kailāsa that you have to give. He died for the treason that he himself committed. And I will not even consider having the traitor back again." [10]

Siriyāla, hearing this fierce outburst, hangs his head in shame. Śiva, for his part, now resorts to another favorite device: in extremis, the god can always reveal his true, divine form. Usually—like the great epiphany at the end of the book of *Job*—this has the effect of putting an end to any unwelcome arguments on the part of the devotees, or of transposing the interaction to a higher metaphysical plane. But in this case, even this shocking revelation cannot move Nimmavva from her stubborn stance:

"Say now! What is the meaning of this, my lord? Is this the kind of thing you are supposed to be doing? Great soul, is this what a great soul should be doing? Do not be mistaken and think that you can distract Nimmavva the way a mother tries to make her child forget her breast by giving him a piece of rice candy. The body fits the life breath, and the life breath fits the body. And I do not want to leave you who have the form of both *liṅga* and *jaṅgama*. Why should I indulge in moods that lead to delusion? Won't the devo-

10. Narayana Rao (1990), 149.

tees laugh at both of us if we succumb to these deceits? Why do you have all these many forms? Did I ever look at you with the slightest bit less favor because of your form? You may have three eyes or you may have no eyes. You may appear in the form of Hara or in the form of a human being. Aren't you still my guru as long as you are associated with the supreme guru? Black Neck, why are you confused? I don't think of you as separate from me, and there is nothing to be afraid of. . . . So stop these tricks! I am wise to all of them. Take whatever form you like, but I am going to feed you."[11]

Śiva clearly has no choice; he starts to eat. He has, at least, made his point to Siriyāla, whose misplaced pride has evaporated. Still, the god wants to bring the usual form of closure to this episode; he revives Nimmavva's son and sends him to Kailāsa. But the mother, true to her fiery temperament, refuses to join him there: she prefers to stay on earth where she can serve the *jaṅgamas*.

There is yet another episode to come; but let us stop for a moment with Nimmavva, to see how her story reflects on the significance of the Siriyāla base-text. Clearly, Siriyāla's sacrifice has been dwarfed by an even more extreme and fanatical act of devotion; the parent's violence against a child is taken to the limit, while the living connection to the deity is, in effect, absolutized (at the expense of any "normal" maternal feeling). But the inner nature of this connection has also been radically reformulated. In effect, Nimmavva establishes a position of superiority, even control, over Śiva, whom she ultimately forces to consume her food. (Note that in this respect, she succeeds where Ciṟuttŏṇṭar fails!) This is the theme of the devotee's autonomy and power over his god, which we saw, in a far milder form, in the Tamil version of the story; in the *BP* generally, this theme is literalized, intensified, and made central. Basava takes a vow never to let Śiva win (in his ongoing contests with him), not even in a dream;[12] Bĕjja Mahādevi—in some ways the closest figure to Nimmavva in the *Basavapurāṇamu*—actually forces a reluctant Śiva to nurse at her breast.[13]

So Nimmavva has the upper hand. Her successful feeding of the

11. Ibid.
12. *BP* 2, 31–32.
13. *BP* 3, 77–80.

deity, against his will, is no metaphor but rather a concrete sign of the ultimate domestication of the mythic being. The god even becomes, in some sense, dependent on this woman, who cannot be swayed from her unqualified truth. Listen to the simile *she* proposes: "Do not be mistaken and think you can distract Nimmavva the way a mother tries to make her child forget her breast by giving him a piece of rice candy." The nursing metaphor is wholly on target: not only does it set up an implicit contrast between the mother's love for her child and the devotee's far more compelling love for god, but it also suggests this strangely inverted dependence of the god on the woman. Śiva, showing his true form in order to avoid eating, is compared to the mother who hides her breast; Nimmavva, by the same token, becomes the single-minded feeder who won't let the god-child escape his meal. The nurturing force she directs at him is denied to her human child. At the same time, the harsh image of weaning—rice-candy substituting for breast-milk—points to the rough-and-ready relationship that this hard-hearted mother establishes with this god.

We can go a step farther with this image. Is it by chance that this blatant subversion of the Tamil paradigm is accomplished by a woman, more precisely, a mother? In effect, the "breast" that the god denies, in Nimmavva's metaphor, is Nimmavva's own breast, bursting with milk that she is determined to feed to her slippery antagonist. But, in this inverted world, this woman can fulfill her maternal function only after first destroying its natural human object and then coercing the divinity into assuming the position she intends for him. Her method is deliberate and unequivocal: where Ciṟuttŏṇṭar appears to be merely playing, rather amateurishly, at this type of mothering, Nimmavva pursues her passion to the end, thereby infantilizing an increasingly helpless deity. There is no question here of a feminine softening or opening or ripening awareness, of an innerness so deep it can sustain savage loss and no less savage paradox. Nimmavva, unlike both Ciṟuttŏṇṭar and *his* wife, has wholly transcended such sentimental states; she has long ago achieved the transformation in consciousness that the Tamil text posits as the devotee's goal. From this vantage point, in the Vīraśaiva context, her lowly status—a lone but independent woman, seemingly even without a husband—becomes an advantage, almost a guarantee of the power and efficacy of her faith. Recall that she mocks the god for assuming he can fool her *because she is a woman,* whereas, in fact, the contrary is rather the case—as a woman, she humiliates and overpowers *him*. We thus encounter a mother who is active, decisive, and potentially destructive toward both the human and the divine. It is as if the ironic undermining of themes of nurturance, with which the Tamil text begins, could only be taken to its final limit through the image of just such a mother, whose entire being is committed to this form of uncompromising awareness.

Note that the incongruous tone so characteristic of Cekkiḻār's version is wholly absent here. The issue is not the paradoxical conjunction of love and heartless slaughter: Nimmavva's act of violence is simply one more in an endless series recounted by this exceedingly violent text. In this series, Ciṟuttŏṇṭar-Siriyāla occupies a place far from the top: "Do you mistake me for Siriyāla?" asks Nimmavva, almost in mockery. This is not only because she has gone beyond his deed in a formal way, first by killing her son, at her own initiative, for a trivial offense, then by refusing to let the god revive him. The real crux is in the meaning of this refusal, especially in relation to the earlier story. Nimmavva indignantly rejects Śiva's offer to restore her son because she abhors its implications. She cannot accept the deviousness, the pathetic inconsistency of the god's tricks: "Do you think you can get by with this just because I am a woman? I know your magic, and I am not stupid." The god, already reduced to helpless subservience, has to be saved from his own inconstancy, from his degrading incarnations in icon and story. She will never allow him to ruin the purity of her act by reversing its consequences; nor will she let the god give meaning to the sacrifice by turning it into some form of test or demonstration, on his terms. What kind of god is it, she seems to be asking, who would stoop to such a trial—apparently out of some inner need of *his?* She, certainly, has no need to collude in such a farce. The child was killed for a reason, and she has no interest in undermining that cause; nor is she attracted in the least to the empty compensations of life in heaven, a reward that Śiva is only too quick to offer, usually as a means of getting himself off the hook.

There is an ontic aspect to this stand. Nimmavva is mercifully spared the Tamil devotee's quandary about Śiva's presence-through-absence. She knows exactly where he is: "I don't think of you as separate from me." Access to the god is no longer a problem; he is securely rooted in the self, monistically identified with the self. The Tamil devotee's residual personhood establishes the conditions for the zigzag interaction with divinity that we observed in the previous chapter; there, sacrifice is necessary to breach the inherently paradoxical boundary between in and out, between human ego and divine other, in a transformative process that includes a culminating reversal of its initial stage. But for the Vīraśaiva saint, this boundary is far less problematic; the devotee literally holds the god in his hand, and can compel his actions and reactions. The ultimate is no longer an elusive and alien other, lurking just beyond awareness, but an entirely familiar and domesticated being, so close and real as to preclude any thought of compromising one's commitment to him. Only *he,* when embodied in his play, is in danger of introducing forms of compromise, from which his servants must now save him. Nimmava achieves this result by asserting the categorical and irreversible nature of her act of sacrifice; the deed speaks for itself, and for the absolute nature of the values that prompt it.

By this logic, however, Siriyāla's story is subjected to an explicit critique. Compared to Nimmavva, both Siriyāla and Śiva are cast in an almost ludicrous light. The whole force of the Siriyāla story has been blunted, its paradigmatic value impaired, its dynamic of faith and testing corroded, perhaps even scorned. But this is only the beginning. The emerging critique is both immeasurably strengthened and developed in a somewhat different direction in the immediate sequel to Nimmavva's story.

3

Halāyudha

Śiva has yet another surprise in store for Siriyāla—a surprise that will boomerang on the god as well. Taking Siriyāla by the hand, Śiva leads him to the village where a certain Halāyudha lives. Halāyudha warmly welcomes these two Śaiva devotees and asks them whence they have come. Siva replies: "We are constantly visiting the *jaṅgamas;* there is no devotee's house that I have not entered. I was born in a place called "No-People-Town" (Nirāḷapuram), but I know nothing of any earthly father or mother. Nimmavva carried me, nursed me, and raised me. . . . The day before yesterday I went to Siriyāla's house, where I saw his son and became friends with this man." And he proceeds to tell Halāyudha, in short, the story of Siriyāla's sacrifice.[14]

He seems to expect Halāyudha to be overcome with admiration for this extreme act of devotion. Instead, Halāyudha reacts with anger and disbelief: "What is this that you are trying to tell me? Is Śiva really a man-eating demon? And is the good devotee, Siriyāla, so devoid of devotion that he would treat his own son like an animal? You are great men, and thus your words cannot be false, but is such a thing possible?"[15]

The disguised Śiva assures him that it is, indeed, that millions of devotees had offered the god their wives, and billions had given him their children. An even greater number had offered up themselves. The god, wishing to test Siriyāla, asked for the thing that was hardest to give, and the father did not hesitate. As a result, people sing the story of Siriyāla in all the villages of the world, and long *kāvyas,* in prose and poetry, are composed on this theme. Siriyāla is the hero of dramas, and his act is sung at the mortar and pestle and at the grinding stone.[16]

At this, Halāyudha is wholly enraged:

"Why did this have to happen? What made Hara (= Śiva) ask for meat, and why did the merchant, Ciṟutŏṇḍa, serve his son? How can a lover of devotees eat a devotee? If Ciṟutŏṇḍa himself were a devotee, how could he kill a devotee? Hara! Hara! Most

14. In this synopsis of the story, we hear for the first time of a twenty-one-days' rain in Kāñci, after which Śiva came down to ask Siriyāla for his son. Earlier, Siriyāla offered sugarcane juice to the devotees, and whatever else they desired; Śiva sent him these devotees "to find out what was in Siriyāla's heart." We will see these elements recurring, in fuller form, in Śrīnātha's fifteenth-century version of the story. See Narayana Rao (1990), 152.

15. Ibid.

16. Note this reference, undoubtedly reliable, to the existence of popular versions of the story; Somanātha may be assumed to have known some such variants.

certainly such a lord and such a devotee are very extraordinary! And you can be sure that there are no others who are like them. How could a child live if his mother were a demoness? Alas! Śiva himself has become a demon! Is it right for him to lose control of himself like this and follow his passions in his ripe old age? And as for this man, it looks as if he developed the usual greed associated with being a merchant and killed his own son out of a desire to satisfy it. To begin with, devotees never touch meat! So why would a devotee feed it to others? And then, why would people glorify such a person? Of course, there is nothing wrong with wanting to discover the depths of the man's devotion. But if Mṛḍa (= Śiva) had any sense, couldn't he have given his approval as soon as Siriyāla lifted the knife to kill his son? Not only that, if this Ciṟutŏṇḍa were actually an intelligent devotee, would he have been willing to kill his son and save himself? But no, he still held onto his own life. Even if the boy were his own son, he was a jaṅgama, wasn't he? How could he possibly kill a jaṅgama like that without any qualms?

"If there is a fire in your neighbor's house, your own house may catch fire. But if there is already a fire in your own house, what can possibly save it? There is a little saying that the outer grief does not affect the inside. So this is how devotion should be! Can't Mṛḍa stomach anything besides human flesh? If Siriyāla had such devotion to Īśvara, why didn't he have himself cooked up and served to Black Neck? How can this be construed as anything but an act of violence against a devotee?

"Then, of course, fearing that he would be blamed for hurting the son and deceiving the father, Śiva ordered the parents to call him. But, then, why didn't Ciṟutŏṇḍa reply that he had just sacrificed the boy and that it was improper to call him back?

"After all this begging and killing, Śiva must have been afraid that he would be viewed as a devouring beast. And so what did he do? He regurgitated the son! And all that after he had eaten his belly full, belching loudly as he did so!

"So the merchant got himself some karma, and the lord has brought a curse upon himself! Isn't that right? This is my response to that! May the demon who ate a devotee, and the butcher who killed a devotee and all those countless ignoramuses who write stories about it be excommunicated along with those who read them."[17]

Perhaps only in India, perhaps only in Andhra, can a devotee bound in intimate worship to a god choose to exclude that god from his own community. Moreover, in this case, the bold excommunicator, Halāyudha, becomes a hero to his tradition: Śiva is so cowed by the devotee's curse that he turns to his wife, Umā, for help; Umā and Sangaḷavva, Siriyāla's wife, are reduced to begging Halāyudha to relent and cancel his imprecation. When, at last, he agrees to do so, Śiva—now readmitted to the society of devotees—embraces him and praises his intelligence, courage, and stubborn certainty. Halāyudha is then rapidly removed to Kailāsa. The god, apparently, is taking no more chances.

Halāyudha shows us the other side of the Vīraśaiva reaction to the Siriyāla story. If Nimmavva overshadows the story by an even more horrific deed, Halayudha recoils from it in protest and disgust. Nothing, it seems, can justify this tale in his eyes. It is all very well to think in terms of a trial; the god has the right to test his servants' devotion—but, asks Halāyudha, almost as if he had read *Genesis* 22, why couldn't he stop the father at the last minute, once his readiness and commitment had been made clear? Why go through with the whole gruesome process (which Halāyudha sees as including a stage of actually devouring, and then regurgitating, the sacrifice)? Both parties seem almost to have enjoyed this repugnant affair, which, in Halāyudha's eyes, is simply a crime, and a foolish, totally unnecessary crime at that. This exercise in demonic cannibalism has no place in *his* form of Śaivism; even to tell the story is an act of evil. There are no extenuating circumstances, no mitigating insights into the strange entanglement of intimacy and violence, no seductive paradoxes of the boundary; the transformative effects of sacrifice upon consciousness are of no interest or account; and the consequences and implications of this deed of terror are perceived as irreversible. If such is the nature of God, then let him be cast out together with his cruel collaborators and willfully blind disciples.

17. Narayana Rao (1990), 153–54.

And there is more. Vīraśaivism is a movement of protest, directed against existing institutions, orthodox concepts, ritual practices; but here protest has spread and turned against the Śaiva deity himself. In essence, this text of violent reversals has reversed the very motif of testing or trial that it itself introduced: it is no longer primarily Siriyāla who is being tested, but Śiva, the hapless deity who is driven to this unacceptable point. The test is truly Śiva's, and the god is seen as having failed it. He, apparently, is the one who is tortured by doubt and the ambiguity of the love relationship; he needs to explore the depths of this relationship, usually in a cruel, manipulative way. Here the price of intimacy is the devotee's continued tolerance of Śiva's ruinous anxiety. But even this is beyond Halāyudha's limit: he resents the need to assuage the god's anxiety, or to put up with his capriciousness; to him, the sacrifice is redundant, its perpetrators traitors to the tradition, its essence demonic horror. No resort to the notion of an ontic hierarchy, in which the divine level, by definition, has prerogatives and powers beyond question, can affect this argument, this critical inversion of the test.

Like Nimmavva, Halāyudha stands his ground. *She* scorns the attempt to undo the sacrifice, or to "read" it within an extraneous frame of reference determined by the god and his needs; *he,* Halāyudha, rejects the very existence of these needs, or, at any rate, their murderous externalization at the devotee's expense. If the god insists on inflicting his suffering on us, we, his human servants, can exile him from our love. The devotee's autonomy is heightened to the point of violence against the very object of his devotion. Moreover, whichever way we go—with Nimmavva's categorical imperative, or with Halāyudha's ethicized perspective—we find that Siriyāla/Ciṟuttŏṇṭar has been relegated to a lower rung. The Tamil tale about the paradoxical mutuality of desire (and its dreadful price) has developed into a rather negative model, in which both deity and devotee are castigated for substantial failures and corrupted awareness. This left-hand version of the text, by reframing it in these ways, successfully eliminates the paradox: values are absolutized and rendered context-free; the human side of the *bhakti* relationship becomes fully autonomous, committed to consistency and a kind of harsh, even fanatical, literalism; the god, identified as nondifferent from the self, is domesticated, internalized, shamed, compelled, expelled. His freedom and playfulness have been largely transferred to the human side of the relation; this switch in roles, or in the balance of forces, allows the violence that initially issued from *him* to reverse its direction and its latent meaning. Śiva is by now the more vulnerable party, easily conquered, even victimized, by the men and women who worship him.

4

Śrīnātha's version

The Siriyāla story lived on in Andhra, as it did in the Tamil south; its restatement and recontextualization in the Vīraśaiva poem of Pālkuriki Somanātha by no means exhausted its fascination or its challenge. In the late fourteenth or early fifteenth century, the great Telugu poet Śrīnātha took it up again in his *kāvya* devoted to Śaiva myths, the *Haravilāsamu*. Our story has pride of place, as the opening narrative, in this delightful work. Notice the title: the trial of Siriyāla is now a *vilāsa*—a romantic amusement—of Śiva (Hara). The term is important, and we will return to it: it conjures up a context of light, erotic play, with connotations of intimacy, imaginative projection, and aesthetic charm. One might not immediately suspect that our painful Tamil story was susceptible to interpretation in this vein; nevertheless, Śrīnātha has almost magically transformed the text, and his version is surely the most lyrical and beautiful of all surviving South Indian ones. It is not easy to convey this beauty, so heavily dependent on texture, in an English summary; the innovations in frame and narrative are really the least of it, although they are the most accessible to "translation" and analysis. We will give attention to these areas, but, particularly in the case of Śrīnātha, the reader should bear in mind Mandelstam's dictum: where a poem can be paraphrased, there poetry has not spent the night; the sheets have not been rumpled.[18]

Śrīnātha was a Brahmin poet, basically aligned with the "high," heavily Sanskritized literary tradition in Telugu (although he has strong links to the folk tradition as well). In some ways the most creative figure in the whole classical period, he represents the

18. Mandelstam (1977), 3.

emergence of Telugu *kāvya* to a new maturity: his impact on diction, style, and the articulation of the poetic line was enormous, and underlies the achievement of his great successors from the sixteenth century. In terms of the artistic refashioning of inherited narrative materials, like the Siriyāla story, he has no equal. But this process of reworking older sources also has a particular historical aspect: Śrīnātha's period was one of institutional consolidation in Andhra Hinduism, as *purāṇic* and Brahminical ideology attained classical literary form in Telugu. Śrīnātha's own *purāṇas* (especially the *Bhīmeśvarapurāṇamu* on Dākṣārāma in the Godāvarī Delta) bear witness to this process, as does the Vaiṣṇava foundation text, the Telugu *Bhāgavatamu,* of his contemporary Potana.[19] The Vīraśaiva challenge had obviously been met, and the dominance of Brahminical norms was more secure, especially in the coastal region—where the *Haravilāsamu* was composed (for the merchant-patron Avaci Tippayya Sĕṭṭi of Nĕllūru). It is in this light that we must view the transformation this poet worked on older Śaiva materials, which he certainly knew in their earlier forms: for example, he actually quotes the Telugu *Basavapurāṇamu* in the course of retelling our story, although he takes the story in an utterly different and unexpected direction. In short, if Cekkiḻār shows us a Veḷāḷa vision, and the *Basavapurāṇamu* a left-hand, heterodox one, Śrīnātha gives us a Brahminized reading of the same basic text.

As with Somanātha, his method involves a liberal and innovative reworking of the frames. Here, in fact, the frames multiply from the start: in the outermost one, we have the poet, Śrīnātha, telling the story to his patron, the Nĕllūru merchant; but then a new, typically *purāṇic* context is provided, in which our hero first assumes a celestial identity. It all begins with the ever-irate sage Durvāsas in his wilderness retreat, the Badarikāśrama. One day the sage is feeding the gentle fawns with the remains of his sacrifices when the heavenly being *(pramatha)* Tumburu flies past, together with his wife, on their way from Kailāsa to worship Śiva at Gokarṇa. Seeing this marvel of affection *(vātsalya),* the rash Tumburu snaps his fingers in amazement, and the fawns, hearing the noise, are startled and run away. This is enough to make Durvāsas

19. See Shulman (in press a).

curse Tumburu and his wife to suffer the common fate of those immortals who cross a sage: they are to undergo the indignity of being born from a human womb. In a panic, Tumburu throws himself at Durvāsas' feet and begs forgiveness; after all, his fault was very slight, and unintentional. Since the sage's word cannot be rendered vain, he, Tumburu, has a series of requests: let him at least be born in the home of someone devoted to Śiva; may his curse have an end, and, until that moment, may his wife remain with Durvāsas in the ashram. All this is granted: "You have committed this mistake which brought on misfortune and aroused my anger; now let this woman stay with me like my own daughter-in-law, while you go and return, like waking after sleep." At once Tumburu is born in a merchant's household in the sacred city of Kāñci, in the Draviḍa land. Named Ciṟutŏṇḍa Nambi, he grows up devoted to Śiva; he marries Tiruvĕṅganāñci, a partial embodiment *(aṃśa)* of his original *apsaras*-wife; they have a son, named Siriyāla.[20] The parents spend their days caring for the *jaṅgamas*.[21]

So Ciṟutŏṇḍa Nambi is none other than the *pramatha* Tumburu reborn, as the result of Durvāsas' characteristic overreaction, in a Tamil home. Moreover, this earthly birth is limited in time and, still more significantly, in real suffering: Tumburu will eventually regain his freedom, "as if waking from sleep." The story, which we already know to be a *vilāsa,* a romantic caprice, is not far removed from a dream. Once born on earth, the exiled *pramatha* will have to undergo mundane forms of experience, for better or worse; but the ultimate ground of these experiences exists on a higher, more abstract plane, where modes of divine playfulness and fantasy have their natural setting. In a sense, the difficult story we know from the Tamil tradition will thus become a compelling, highly emotional, always aesthetically satisfying projection from this realm of divine playfulness into the reduced existential sphere of the human world. The trick, so to speak, will be to retain this awareness even under conditions which would seem certain to destroy it.

20. Note how Śrīnātha reverts here to the original name of the child in Tamil (Cīrāḷaṉ = Siriyāla), unlike the *BP,* where Siriyāla is a name of the *father,* Ciṟuttŏṇṭar.

21. Note how this Vīraśaiva term is absorbed by our Brahminical text, which uses it to refer to Śaiva devotees.

The *purāṇas* love such a frame, in which each protagonist has an earlier, divine identity, usually forgotten within the limits of a clouded human awareness but ultimately reestablished and regained. Such stories then form a cycle: from heaven to earth, and back to heaven.[22] To some extent, the cycle "cushions" the painful aspects of the framed episodes on earth. But, true both to his general programme and to the hints embedded in the *BP* (or another earlier version), this poet provides yet another, even softer and more charming cushion. For we have one more introductory episode that seeks to explain, from another angle, Śiva's testing of Ciṟutŏṇḍa Nambi:

One day a *miṇḍa jaṅgama*—a "playboy ascetic"—comes to Ciṟutŏṇḍa and asks him for sugarcane juice to bathe his god (in the form of a *liṅga*). At once the Little Devotee rushes off to the market, where he purchases one hundred stalks of sugarcane, without bargaining or arguing. But he is unable to lift this heavy burden, which he needs to take home to the sugarcane press. Seeing him staggering under the weight, Śiva himself hastens there, lifts the stalks, and carries them to Ciṟutŏṇḍa's house.

So far so good. Yet all this happens while the god, in his proper form and home on Mount Kailāsa, is watching a performance of the heavenly dancing girls. Beside him sits Pārvatī, his wife. As the concert proceeds, Śiva begins to sweat profusely since, after all, part of him is hard at work in torrid Kāñci, with the stalks of sugarcane. Pārvatī notices this, and misinterprets it: surely it is a sign of her husband's awakening desire for the dancing girls. In jealousy and anger, she strikes him with the lotus she holds in her hand; pollen spills into the god's three eyes. Blinking madly, and smiling in spite of this assault, he chides his wife:

> What are you thinking, my love?
> Isn't half my body yours?
> Are our hearts not neighbors?
> We two are as one: how, then,
> could my heart hide any feeling
> it might have

22. See Blackburn (1987); note that even the Tamil *Pĕriya Purāṇam* follows this pattern, giving its central hero, Nampi Ārūraṉ, an original appearance in Śiva's heaven. See Shulman (1990), xxvii–xxviii.

from yours?
There is not the least
reason for suspicion:
don't be alarmed, accept
the truth.
You have struck me for nothing,
with a spray of pollen and honey,
and now my eyes
are full of tears. (1.27)

But still he must explain, and he does so just a little too much, not aware of the mistake he is making. "Of all the islands making up the world," he says, "the Jāmbu Island is the best; in it, the Bharata realm is best; the Draviḍa land surpasses all others there, and Kāñcipuram is at the very center—the encircling belt *(kāñcidhāmamu)*—of that land. In that city, there is a merchant, Ciṟutŏṇḍaśreṣṭhuḍu, who is the best of all devotees. No one on earth can equal him; he supplys the *jaṅgamas* with whatever they desire, even at the risk of his life. His heart is a bedchamber for Ekāmranātha and Ambikā.[23] A *jaṅgama* came to him and asked for sugarcane juice; when he could not manage by himself to lift the huge burden of stalks, I went to help him. He pushed from his side, and I from the other; he perspired, and so did I. That is what you saw: you know I am always doing such little favors *(canuvulu)* for my devotees. I love them, and they love me."

Let us take a moment to notice this term: *canuvu* is a form of intimate giving, an act of friendship that transcends normal constraints on interaction, that reflects a commitment rooted in deep affection. It is a key word for this version of the story; the *vilāsa,* Śiva's play, is here explained not in terms of the god's hunger for sensual experience, as in Cekkiḻār, but in terms of this free and familiar linkage between friends. Certainly, the word—along with the rest of the explanation—works strongly upon Pārvatī, who, predictably, demands to see this wonder, this hero servant of Śiva *(av vīramāheśvarun)*. And, after all this, the god clearly has little choice but to fulfill his wife's request.

Here, then, is the third frame, that is meant to provide the immediate context for Śiva's descent to Kāñci. Implicit in it is a some-

23. Śiva at Kāñcipuram, and his consort.

what muted notion of testing, as if Pārvatī couldn't quite believe her husband's inflated claims about this man. Beyond that, however, we should notice the light erotic coloring of this frame, entirely proper to the term *vilāsa;* in effect, a familiar type of lovers' quarrel, in heaven, sets the god in motion toward this world. This is an altogether different type of setting, and a different mode of playing, from what we have seen up till now; we might speak even of a *vilāsic* ontology, in which events ultimately transpire on a level of dream-like fantasy lightly seasoned with sensual desire. Such an ontology of action goes a long way toward redefining the meaning of the sacrifice that is in store.

Meanwhile, Śiva has ordered Indra, god of storms, to rain down a deluge upon Kāñcipuram; for twenty-one days, the torrents never cease. There is method to this attack on the city: Śiva has, so he informs Indra, "some secret to be accomplished" (*galadu māku rahasyakāryam' ŏkaṭi,* 2.15). The final result of the incessant rains is a mass exodus from Kāñci of all ascetics, in their rich variety of classes and beliefs—Buddhists, Jainas, Pāṣaṇḍas, Lokāyatikas, Cārvākas, Kāpālikas, Āhituṇḍikas, Vānaprasthas, Pāśupatas, Jaṅgamayogis—in short, all feedable Śaivas as well as other groups. For his part, Ciṟutŏṇḍa Nambi has gone on feeding whomever he could find, even burning his rich silk cloths, soaked in oil, when no firewood was left for cooking the food. But at last the day arrives when, although the rains have finally ceased, he cannot find a single Śaiva devotee to feed. Usually, thousands would throng to his doorstop; now there is no one, and he must wander the streets in a desperate search, like someone looking for cows that have lost their way, or for money that has fallen from his hand (2.45). He covers all the neighborhoods of Kāñci, the bazaar, the temples, the taverns and gambling houses, the public spaces, the courtesans' dwellings—to no avail. At length he leaves the fortified, enclosed area of the city and wanders into the gardens and fields outside. There, lying on the porch of an old, ruined temple, is an old man, his body broken with age and eaten away by leprosy, his hairs white, his forehead marked with the Śaiva sign of burnt ash; his wife, aged and blind, is massaging his feet.

This is Ciṟutŏṇḍa's opportunity. "Come worship Śiva [by eating] in my house," he asks, bowing to the couple. The old man can hardly hear, but he eventually replies: "What is your family? Tell me your name. Will your wife listen to you? Do you have children? Can you give me what I ask? And why should I bother you as a beggar, whoever you are? It's enough for me if you have the courage to perform a heroic Śaiva vow. But why waste words? I will tell you my wish. I have taken on myself a frightful vow to go without food for a long time, as I worship Śiva. An animal sacrifice must mark the end of this vow, and it can be no other animal than a human child, from a Brahmin, Kṣatriya, or Vaiśya family. He must be healthy and beautiful; his father and mother must first perform his thread-ceremony (of initiation), then cook and serve him; after offering to Śiva, I will eat him, while you and your son sit beside me and eat as well [or, changing the syntax: while you eat your son!]."[24]

Ciṟutŏṇḍa Nambi, of course, accepts this request; he introduces himself by name and explains the vow *he* has taken—to help the devotees achieve their vows, or to kill himself if he fails in this. But the old man is still somewhat skeptical: "You had better go and ask your wife. It is too far for me to go to your house and back, and she may not agree: the mother carries the child in her womb, gives birth to him in pain, cleans up his wastes. . . . Love for a son is no ordinary thing. You have never experienced such horrible vows as this. Let your wife accept first, and then you; if husband and wife do not speak with one voice, this dharma cannot work. Moreover,

> You may be prepared to kill,
> in the firmness of your vow,
> and the mother, out of courage,
> might even bear it,
> and as for me—I might just be able
> to eat that food
> in the intensity of my desire—
> but for a little boy, dying
> is very hard. (2.63)

Obedient to the old man's wishes, Ciṟutŏṇḍa Nambi rushes home. As he expects, his wife is not at all disturbed; she even smiles gently as she assures him, "Our god, the life in our bodies, is identical with the Śivayogis. Is it so great a thing to give him

24. *nā paṅktin īvu nī kŏḍukū guḍuva,* 2.54.

back what is already his? If he wanted, he could eat us together with our son." So all is agreed: husband and wife are united in this endeavor *(ekodyogambu);* Ciṟutŏṇḍa Nambi goes off to bring the aged devotee to his house.

While he is on his way, two short episodes of testing are introduced. This is an innovation in Śrīnātha, a transposition of the trial-motif from the father (as in the *Basavapurāṇamu* version), or the god and the father together (as in Halāyudha's critique in that same text) to the son and the mother, both of whom now assume a much expanded role. First, Śiva takes a different form and goes to visit the child, Siriyāla, at his school, "in order to shake his mind" *(madi jalimpã gã).* He finds the boy learning to read and write, practising a hymn of praise to Śiva. As the child bows to him, the disguised ascetic says, "Your father is that evil-minded Ciṟutŏṇḍa Nambi; he has just promised some drunken Yogi that he will kill you and serve you to him for a meal. I have come to tell you this, out of affection for you. What kind of a father is that? He must be a demon *(dānavuḍu).* Remember the Vedic saying, *jīvan bhadrāṇi paśyati*—you have to be alive to see auspicious things. Take it to heart, run away somewhere, save yourself."

The boy covers his ears with his hands.

> "Is it right for someone like you,
> flawless in deed,
> to speak like this?
> I would hesitate to speak against you
> if I didn't know
> that to spend the wealth of one's body
> for the good of another
> is the only reason to be born. (2.79)

Why should we feel sorry about giving up this impermanent, filthy body to help another person, thus winning a body of fame *(kīrtikāyambu)* that endures for aeons?"

So the intended sacrifice is actually a kind of bargain, in the eyes of its intended victim! The god—"the puppeteer who pulls the strings in this beguiling drama of life" *(kapaṭamāyāmahānāṭakaprapañcasūtradhāruṇḍu)*—is suitably impressed. "This child is even more [firm? devoted? crazy?] than his father!" One test has been passed.

Meanwhile, Pārvatī is paying a visit to Tiruvĕṅganāñci, the boy's mother. The goddess appears as a sixteen-year-old girl, who has just given birth and who wants more milk for her baby. Her own nipples are swollen with milk, but Tiruvĕṅganāñci gives her more; and, in this liquid, maternal setting, the goddess says: "People everywhere, in all the lanes and alleys, are saying that you're about to kill your son for the sake of some evil Yogi *(dur-nirvāṇi)*. You know these Yogis—they'll do anything for the sake of gaining powers *(nidhānanavasiddhulakai)*, in their impudence and deceit. It isn't right to kill a child. If a person puts even a tiny bit of sacred ash on his body, he gets crazy as a pumpkin. Your husband is blind; who the hell is he to kill your son? As the proverb says, 'Is he a man or a tree?' *(magavāḍo mrāṇo)*."

But Tiruvĕṅganāñci pays no heed. "There is no difference between Śiva and the Śivayogi. It's getting late, your breasts are filling with milk, your baby will be in need. You had better go and come again." One mother to another: the striking fact is that, despite the explicit reference to the aggression that is soon to come, one hardly feels it; the very words are coated in milk, they issue softly from the speaker's mouth; this trial, like all the other events described in this version, passes gently, dreamily, in the sweet musical intoxication of the Telugu verse. This is Śrīnātha's miraculous power, used in a premeditated manner to mitigate—actually, to "liquid-ate", to wash away entirely—the elements of horror and incongruity that linger in this tale. In this way, filicide becomes almost a peaceful nursing scene, a stolen kiss, a happy game.

It is a powerful and consistent transformation, that reaches its apogee in the next, concluding scene. Ciṟutŏṇḍa Nambi has carried the old leper home on his back, as the blind old lady limps along beside him.[25] A clear Brahminical element is worked in at this point: Ciṟutŏṇḍa Nambi insists (in accordance with the Yogi's original condition) that their son have his thread-ceremony *(va-ḍugu = upanayana)* before he is sacrificed. This is quickly accom-

25. Note this eloquent image of the devotee unconsciously carrying his god on his back. Śrīnātha tells us that people who saw this strange sight were overcome with emotion and cried out the many names of Śiva; and the poet himself cannot refrain from saying, in his own name: "If one thinks of it, what marvelous good fortune was this, to carry the god, that false Bhairava, on his back through the streets!" (2.89).

plished; the boy is fetched from school, fed, bathed and adorned in his finest. Now his parents can inform him what is about to happen, and they do so in a remarkable verse, quite devoid of any sense of incipient violation:

> So that a certain Bhairava Yogi
> who follows the Pāśupata vow
> can break his fast,
> we are preparing you,
> beloved son,
> as a meat repast.
> We hope you have no hesitation,
> not even a little,
> inside your heart
> about leaving behind you
> this dizzying world. (2.111)[26]

And Siriyāla responds in equally gentle and accepting tones: "I haven't the least attachment to *saṃsāra;* please don't be upset; I am happy to become food for that false Yogi, that Śiva *(śivunakun māyāmahāyogikin).*[27] I beg you, my parents, have no fear of committing an act of injury *(hiṃsākleśamu).*"

As if giving him her breast, the mother holds her son on her thighs; the maid, Candanikā, places a vessel underneath; the boy, smiling a little, folds his hands in prayer; Ciṟutŏṇḍa sharpens his knife. Their hearts are united, without sorrow. When the head falls, it is still chanting the *mantra,* "Homage to Śiva!" The smile is still on Siriyāla's face; his features have the beauty of a child falling asleep (*nidra vovunaṭl' andamun ŏndĕn,* 2.119). If we didn't know the story—if we were reading or hearing it for the first time—we might almost miss the fact that an act of violence has taken place.

The parents feel as if they had made a wager and won; or as if they had paid off a debt. Time to cook the meal—with pepper, onion, turmeric, asaphoetida, fenugreek, cumin, sugar, tamarind, ghee, oil, and curd, all expertly mixed with the meat that is carefully cut in strips, fried, not overcooked. . . . We can hurry past

26. *nī hṛdayambun andu saṃsāramū bāyā jālani vicāramu ledu kadā yŏk' intayun.*

27. Note that the boy seems to be aware of the real identity of the family's guest, and the nature of his disguise.

The mother washes her child to prepare him for the sacrifice. Lepakshi, Andhra Pradesh. Photo: courtesy Yigal Bronner.

this lush description, while taking note of a major point: impossible as it might seem, the fact that a child is being cooked and served is almost irrelevant. We are far beyond the overt aggression of the Tamil *Pĕriya Purāṇam;* moreover, the oral obsession that we discovered there has taken an altogether different form in Śrīnātha—not hunger and its inconceivable satisfaction, not the driving compulsion to feed, but the simple, sensual joy of good food. Śrīnātha is famous for his detailed descriptions of food and eating—he must have loved this part of life—and he was clearly not about to miss a chance for another such lyrical passage even in the somewhat unsettling context of the Siriyāla story.

This matter of taste and spices will appear again, at the very end. In its own way, it beautifully signals the changed tone and direction of this version. A long passage describes the final preparations, the banana-leaf—neither too tender nor too hard—spread to receive the rice and curries, the blessings, the arrangement of the dishes. As we expect, the Bhairava looks at the food and turns away: there is no head-meat; see what comes of the natural attachment to one's son! His vow is ruined, he cannot eat. But the maid has anticipated the fuss that these Yogis always make, and the head-curry is actually ready. Now comes the heart of the demand: "You must sit beside me and eat; the Veda forbids one to eat alone. And there is one thing more: I cannot put food in my mouth unless a child eats near me. I won't eat in the home of a luckless man who has no son. Call your son."

The father answers: "Yes, I forgot. I do have another son. He is probably playing or reading. I'll send for him. But the curries are getting cold: please eat, O best of Yogis."

"Let your wife face the four directions and call the boy. If he comes, we will eat together in the row. If he doesn't, this old wife of mine and I will eat—since we would not want all your work to go to waste." He is considerate, this Śiva of Śrīnātha's: observe how he allays in advance the fundamental anxiety that torments Ciṟutŏṇḍa in the Tamil text, which climaxes at this point. He will eat in any case, but let the mother make her call.

She does so in another exquisite verse combining vocatives and imperatives, which build up to a moving series of synonyms for the word "son":

The mother serves her son to the divine guest. Lepakshi, Andhra Pradesh. Photo: courtesy Yigal Bronner.

Come, come to me, moon rising from the ocean
  of this merchant's family!
Come, your eyes like lotus blossoms
  opening at dawn!
Come, you who follow the grim path of the Śaiva
  heroes!
Come, you have broken through the cycle of empty
  lives . . .
Won't you come, child born from my body,
  Siriyāla, breath of my life?
Won't you come, my little boy? (2.134)

When he comes—first appearing in his mother's mind, then in the flesh[28]—each part of his body is still redolent of the special fragrance of the spices used in preparing that particular dish *(tattad-vyañjanapākagandhyavayavasthānapratānambuton).*

There remains only the final revelation, which restores the exiled *pramatha* to his former station: Śiva informs him of his "real" identity as Tumburu, while his wife resumes her role as *apsaras;* as for Siriyāla, he is none other than Kumārasvāmi, Śiva's own son. In this sense—another example of the neat *purāṇic* closure that this text seeks and achieves—Śiva has all along been asking only for what is truly his.

5

Summary

We have followed Śrīnātha at some length, in the hope that something, at least, of his power and the unique "feel" of his texture might be transmitted in the telling. Most of the major analytical features have been noted as we went along; for now, let me simply summarize them again briefly, before considering the larger picture that has emerged from the Telugu versions.

1. *Texture.* This is still, no doubt, a story of incongruous deeds and emotions, and yet we can say without exaggeration that the sense of incongruity has been wholly eliminated on the level of language and style. The act of violence at the center of the story passes almost unremarked. It is intimated throughout in largely

28. Reading *jittambun gana vaccĕ;* v.l. *jittamb' ubbā gā vaccĕ.*

indirect ways, which soften its contours: thus the parents hope their child has "no hesitation about leaving this dizzying world," as if his translation to another world were a matter of delicate and painless transition, like falling asleep.[29] Śrīnātha's Telugu is a study in sensuous harmonies; there is nothing of the stark juxtapositions we saw in Cekkiḻār; the narration as a whole is bathed in soft and loving tones, which also resonate through the melodic Sanskrit compounds that are deftly woven into the Telugu syntax. Look, for example, at the long compound just quoted, that describes the fragrances still clinging to the revived boy's various limbs: *tat-tad-vyañjana-pāka-gandhy-avayava-sthāna-pratānambuton*. A Telugu instrumental/associative ending links the compound with the main clause of the sentence; the resonant back-vowels, *a* and *ā*, together with the recurrent nasals, create a kind of swelling drone, like the *tambura* base-notes in a concert; the dentals punctuating this musical tone at the two extremities of the compound mark a beat that seems almost to imitate the uneven, accelerating patter of the child's feet as he comes running to his mother's arms. The amazing syntactical compression of the Sanskrit builds the tension in the verse to a climax here, in its concluding line, as the compound strives toward resolution; as so often in Telugu *kāvya*, the transition to a lengthy string of Sanskrit both indicates that we are at a critical point and provides emphatic closure and release. The boy is back: we hear him coming, we feel the rising tide of emotion; the sweet fragrances enveloping his body are subtly, synaesthetically translated into the harmonious patterns of bilingual, verbal sound. Effects such as these are liberally sprinkled throughout Śrīnātha's poems.

2. *Reframing*. The story is set within a series of superimposed frames, which offer a different rationale for what transpires. All the major actors acquire a *purāṇic* identity, which both pervades and transcends their earthly experience. As with the texture, the result is a general softening of the harsh human reality that other versions stress. Ciṟutŏṇḍa Nambi is as if caught up in a dream—and the dream, classed as *vilāsa*, has a seductive and playful quality. The immediate context is Pārvatī's pique at her husband—a

29. As the poet explicitly tells us at 2.119, cited above: Siriyāla's decapitation leaves the boy smiling, with the beauty of a child falling asleep.

conventional erotic theme. Within this setting, Siva defines his relations with Ciṟutŏṇḍa Nambi in terms of a loving familiarity, *canuvu,* that apparently can also explain the "trial" imposed on the devotee. This trial is, however, hardly central to the relationship; the motif of testing, in an explicit way, is transferred to the son and mother, both of whom assume here a far more active role than in earlier versions. Indeed, the son might almost be said to volunteer for this sacrifice,[30] from an inner stance of utmost security, trust, and freedom; this well-articulated awareness, which seems also to reflect the mother's innerness, is itself a kind of reframing through reformulating the emotional premises on which the story rests.

3. *Narrative contours.* Here, too, we see the tendency to soften and reduce. The power politics—so crucial to both the *Pĕriya Purāṇam* and the *Basavapurāṇamu* versions—have disappeared; neither the god nor his devotee is maneuvering for a position of superiority. The anxiety-ridden theme of oral incorporation, which we first observed in Cekkiḻār, is transposed to a straightforward celebration of delicious food. Moreover, the devotee's anxiety about feeding no longer has any place; the god assures him that he will consume the offering even if the child fails to appear. Again, as in *Basavapurāṇamu,* we find a hypertrophied image of nursing—the mother holds the child in her arms, as he is about to be slaughtered, "as if she were giving him her breast"—but here the simile is anything but ironic; the context is truly one of nurturance and love, *despite* the outward aspect of violent sacrifice (which is barely noticed). Tiruvĕṅganāñci, in Śrīnātha's version, thus restores the image of the mother to a more benign perspective; the filicide is truly subsumed by the enveloping atmosphere of maternal nursing, in an almost magical externalization, through subtle narrative and linguistic means, of a sensibility marked primarily by the drive toward selfless giving. (Here one is struck by the emerging contrast with the other mothers we have met—Vĕṇkāṭṭunaṅkai of the Tamil version, whose experience is permeated by the tensions of paradox and violent loss; and Nimmavva of the

30. As does the son of the heroic Vīravara in *Kathāsaritsāgara* 78 and *Hitopadeśa* 3 (after verse 102)—a tale of filicide that does not, however, conform to the *aqedah* type.

Basavapurāṇamu, embodying a fierce maternal persona at once absolutized, traumatizing, and rich in coercive power). Note that Siriyāla, at the end, is identified with Śiva's own son in yet another move away from the more horrific configuration of the original Tamil tale.

4. *Ontology.* Events unfold against a different metaphysical backdrop, which radically changes their significance. This is no longer the realistic universe of Tamil Śaivism; creation, and its consequences, are now largely subsumed within the notion of *vilāsa,* the god's happy play. In the Tamil text, Śiva's play is all too readily linked with a sense of terror; indeed, we saw that this conjunction, together with the third term, *karuṇā*—the god's compassion—constitutes the semantic core of Śaiva psychology in the far south.[31] But in the Brahminized universe of Śrīnātha, the element of terror is much subdued; *vilāsa* is a romantic, lightly eroticized mode not far removed from the realms of fantasy and dream. In a *vilāsic* ontology, there are no irreversible losses, no unhealable pains; one can always resort to a higher, more encompassing level of being, which sustains the more limited level of human identity and awareness. Father, mother, and son are never simply "themselves." Moreover, within this kind of universe the inner movement of "as if"—the assertion of a subjunctive reality experienced on its own terms, within the subjective self—has a truly compelling power, as we see by the way the moment of calling and revival is articulated here. This is clearly the high point of Śrīnātha's text (as it is, in a rather different way, in the *Basavapurāṇamu*); its power over the reader seems bound up with an implicit claim about the superior reality of the inner world of feeling and imagination, as opposed to the somewhat devalued sphere of external deeds. The child is "as if" alive: the mother's call, with its long, compounded vocatives—so concrete and specific—makes sense only in light of this assumption; the sacrifice itself, only dimly present, matters far less than this personal, boldly stated, emotive perception. Although the "as if" reality still has to be corrobo-

31. See above, chapter 2. For further examples of the conjunction of play and violence or terror in *Pĕriya Purāṇam,* see, for example, the story of Caṇṭīcaṉ, the Brahmin boy who cuts off his father's legs when the father attacks the *liṅga* of sand that he has playfully built and playfully worships—as the text explicitly stresses. *PP* 1.4.6, especially verses 32 and 47.

rated and confirmed—the child does return, all flesh and fragrance—the primacy (perhaps we should say the factuality) of the projected wish is fundamental to the *vilāsa*-mode. Needless to say, this is a very different notion from the *Pĕriya Purāṇam*'s theme of externalizing into sensuous reality the latent, potential forms of divine existence. Indeed, the hierarchy of being is reversed in these two cases; in one, the sensually concrete subsumes more abstract, hidden levels; in the other, Brahminical vision, the outer world is but a pale refraction of the inner, imaginative, "as if" projections of the real.

6

The three major versions of the Ciruttŏṇṭar myth that we have studied present us with radically divergent thematics, rooted in varying social and cultural milieux. One way to restate these emerging distinctions is to notice how the narrative climax is articulated differently in each of the texts. Although the moment when the mother calls her son is clearly the culminating point of reversal and transformation in all these versions, we can further unpack its emphases and structure in a comparative light. In the Veḷāḷa version of Cekkiḻār, the greatest intensity attaches to the series of sadistic demands that immediately precedes the mother's call; Ciruttŏṇṭar is slowly brought to the edge of collapse and inextricable paradox, as we hear in his despairing cry: "What can I do to make this man eat?" The child is dead, yet the guest demands that he be called; the overt paradox is vehicle and symbol for the even more fundamentally paradoxical problem of the meeting between god and man—a meeting propelled by mutual and complementary needs, and burdened with an unavoidable propensity for violent sacrifice. This sacrifice, an arena of terror, aggression, and transformation, is the price of intimacy, which both parties seek.

In the left-hand text of Pālkuriki Somanātha, the mother's call is the high point of the Siriyāla story proper; but the most forceful passages, that crystallize the author's standpoint, are found in the containing frames of Nimmavva and Halāyudha. Their tenacious opposition to the god, and to the inherited stories of his hair-raising pranks, best expresses the Vīraśaiva drive toward protest and rebellion. The act of reviving the sacrificial victim, however powerfully portrayed, is now seen as a cheap trick on the part of an untrustworthy partner to the *bhakti* relationship; paradox is rejected, and the hungry god is put to the test. Halāyudha's curse against Śiva and Siriyāla crowns this process of radical revision and, by reversing the value of the Tamil paradigm, suggests the existence of an alternative, left-handed path of devotion—one in which the devotee can always claim the upper hand as the representative of an absolutized conception of god. Here violence is the handmaiden of this uncompromising adherence to an absolute truth.

Finally, in Śrīnātha's text the mother's call is truly the end of the story. The poet has sung away the aspects of killing and terror; the sacrifice exists, in a sense, only in order to be reversed, its losses canceled and forgotten; its real purpose is to trigger the demonstration of subjunctive vision, the emotional projection into the world of the "as if" inner mode. Calling out to her child, the mother successfully plays with the world in the manner of the god, whose *vilāsa* works as a gentle solvent on the harsh lines of the story. Both Ciṟuttŏṇṭar and Śiva have been Brahminized, *purāṇicized,* contained; their driving need for one another is no longer a disruptive, unpredictable collusion on the border of death, but rather an affectionate sharing of favors within a framework of joyful play. The Tamil myth, with all its terror, has been domesticated in the guise of a soothing, lyrical dream.

There are many more versions of this story in the South Indian literary traditions. For example, the Telugu folk-epic, *Palnāṭi vīrula katha*—which speaks of Siriyāla in a long digression from its main concerns—makes the boy's mother (here called Siriyāla Maṅgamma) the central figure; she is the greatest of all devotees in this Kali Age, and is thus the object of the gods' test; she, rather than her husband, slaughters the child, not once but twice—since, upon the boy's reappearance in answer to her call, the disguised Śiva accuses her of having killed someone else's child and demands that the sacrifice be performed again![32] This is a particularly powerful telling keyed to the heroic values of the epic in which it is embedded; as with Nimmavva, a kind of extreme one-

32. See Roghair (1982), 297–307, for a translation of the text.

upmanship—identified with the mother's role—intensifies the violence and extends its meaning. There is a Tamil chapbook, the *Ciṟuttŏṇṭapattaṉ katai,*[33] which has absorbed important elements from the Telugu versions we have studied; and a beautiful, very simply told account, the *Ciṟuttŏṇṭanāyaṉār carittirak kummi,*[34] in one of the prevalent Tamil folk genres (*kummi*). The story is also known in the Kannada tradition. Farther north, there are Sanskrit refractions, fairly distant from the Tamil originals, in the *Tāpīmāhātmya* and *Narmadāmāhātmya,* collections of myths on great rivers of the Deccan.[35] Folktales from as far as Gujarat and Kashmir repeat the story in its essential outline.[36] I have no doubt that further search would produce other examples ultimately derived from our Tamil source, not simply exemplars of the general type. We could, of course, profitably pursue these other versions, searching for the lines of transformation and their rationale; the search would take us deep into layers of the folk tradition, with their unique cosmologies and theologies. But books, especially short books, should have an end. So for the moment, we leave Ciṟuttŏṇṭar to his devotion and turn to a much more ancient tale.

33. Published in Madras by R. G. Pati Kampĕṉi, 1975.

34. (Madras: R. G. Pati Kampĕṉi, 1974). A noteworthy innovation of this version is the theme of the child's dream (or nightmare) of being sacrificed by his father—a dream initially denied by the child's teacher, and then lived out in gruesome actuality.

35. *Tāpīmāhātmya* 58; *Narmadāmāhātmya* 26; see summaries and discussion in Feldhaus (1990).

36. Bose (1977), 67–68, where the setting is Sialbet in Saurastra; Beck et al. (1987), 81–85.

4

Śunaḥśepa: The Riddle of Fathers and Sons

1

By far the most famous case of attempted filicide in Vedic literature is that of Śunaḥśepa, who substitutes for another intended victim named Rohita. In terms of our framework, it is, in fact, Rohita who is closest to the *aqedah* type, as we shall see; but the true hero of the story is the wise child Śunaḥśepa, and it is his role that gives coherence and meaning to the tale. It is not by chance that most later versions refer to it by his name. The story, first fully recorded in the *Aitareya Brāhmaṇa* (7.13–18), lived on in the *Rāmāyaṇa* and the *purāṇas,* which transformed it considerably; more obliquely, it also developed in a rather new direction in the highly popular *purāṇic* tale of Hariścandra, who sells his wife and child into slavery in order to pay a promised debt.[1] We will concentrate on the *Brāhmaṇa* narrative of Śunaḥśepa, its logic and hidden message, its direct descendants in the classical literature,

1. The locus classicus for the purāṇic Hariścandra is *Mārkaṇḍeyapurāṇa* 7–8; elaborate versions exist from the medieval period in both Sanskrit and the regional languages. The unhappy king Hariścandra, father to Rohita or Rohitāsya, clearly resumes the identity of the Hariścandra (father to Rohita) known from the *Brāhmaṇa* texts, and the two stories resonate in fundamental ways. The purāṇic Hariścandra—who also, in some sense, sacrifices his son—deserves a book of his own; precisely for this reason, we cannot explore his story here.

and, very briefly, the suggestive analogies with, and distinctions from, Greek materials.

This is a story of sacrifice not only by virtue of its overt narrative content but also in terms of its place within the Vedic sacrificial cult. The text was recited in the course of the *rājasūya* rituals of royal consecration; indeed, as the *Aitareya Brāhmaṇa* itself states, at the conclusion of the story, reciting this story liberates the newly consecrated king from evil. A victorious king, even when he is not performing sacrifice, should have this story sung, so that not the least bit of evil will remain with him.[2] Here, then, is the first riddle posed by this enigmatic text: why, or how, can it do away with evil? And why is it embedded in this way within the ritual of royal consecration?

Like so many stories, this one begins with a childless king—Hariścandra, a descendant of Ikṣvāku, who had a hundred wives but no son from any of them. This royal figure was host to two sages, Parvata and Nārada, and it was to the latter that the king posed his question:

> Those who know, and those who don't—
> they all want a son.
> What does one find through a son?
> Tell me that, Nārada.

The question, we observe, begins with the theme of knowing or understanding (the verb is *vi-jñā*). The king, who seems to belong with those who fail to know, asks in a single verse; Nārada's enigmatic reply, as the text itself notes, is in ten:

> The father who sees the face of his newborn son, alive, repays his debt and achieves immortality. As great as the joys living beings have on earth, in fire and water—greater than these is the father's joy in his son. Fathers have always crossed through the dense darkness by means of a son, who is a source of comfort: the self is born from the self (*ātmā hi jajña ātmanaḥ*).
>
> Food is the breath of life. Clothing is a refuge. Gold is beautiful form. Cattle are marriage. A wife is a friend, a daughter is misery—but a son is the light in the highest heaven.

2. *Aitareya Brāhmaṇa* 7.18.

The husband enters his wife and becomes an embryo inside her, his mother. Becoming new in her again, he is born in the tenth month. Since he is born (*jāyate*) in her, she is called "wife" (*jāyā*). This is the power (*ābhūti*) that infuses the seed.

The gods and sages brought glory to her; the gods said to men, "Here is your mother." All animals know that he who has no son has no world at all. That is why a son mounts his mother and his sister. This is the wide, easy path traveled painlessly by those who have sons; animals and birds see it, and unite with their mothers.

Now the practical conclusion to this lengthy exposition: "Ask Varuṇa for a son, whom you promise to sacrifice." So Hariścandra prays to Lord Varuṇa: "Let a son be born to me, and I will sacrifice him to you." Varuṇa agrees and a son, Rohita, is born. But when Varuṇa wishes to claim his promised victim, the father puts him off again and again: he will sacrifice him only when he is fit, i.e., after ten days, or when his first teeth appear, or when these deciduous teeth fall out, or when his permanent teeth come in, or when he becomes able to bear arms like the Kṣatriya prince he is. At last the moment can no longer be deferred: Rohita is a grown warrior, and the god demands that the sacrifice take place. The father speaks to his son: "My child, this one gave you to me. Let me now sacrifice you to him." "No," says Rohita and, taking his bow, departs for the forest.

At his departure, his father is seized by Varuṇa and his stomach swells with sickness. For a year, Rohita wanders, until he hears of his father's illness and returns to the village; there he is met by Indra, disguised as a man, who tells him to wander on, "for Indra is the friend of the wanderer." Five times this scenario is repeated: at the end of each year, Rohita returns to the village only to meet the disguised deity, who, speaking in riddle-like metaphors, sends him back to the wilderness. In the sixth year of his wanderings, Rohita comes upon a strange Brahmin family—the father, Ajīgarta Sauyavasi, a hungry man; and his three sons, Śunaḥpuccha, Śunaḥśepa, and Śunolāṅgula ("Dog's Ass," "Dog's Penis," and "Dog's Tail," respectively). Rohita, the intended victim at his father's sacrifice, sees a way out: he offers a hundred cows for one of the boys, who will take his place. The father refuses to part with the eldest son, and the mother clutches the youngest; the middle son, Śunaḥśepa, is sold and sent off with the Kṣatriya boy.

Rohita rushes back to the village and tells his father that he wishes to ransom himself with the Brahmin substitute-victim. Varuṇa accepts the exchange: "A Brahmin is more than a Kṣatriya." The god then teaches Hariścandra the order of the royal consecration *(rājasūyaṃ yajñakratum)*; at the high point of the ritual, the anointing ceremony *(abhiśecanīya)*, Śunaḥśepa is brought forward as a human sacrificial beast *(puruṣaṛ paśum ālebhe)*.

It is a major rite, with famous officiants: Viśvāmitra the *hotṛ*, Jamadagni the *adhvaryu*, Vasiṣṭha the *brahman*, Ayāsya the *udgātṛ*. But, at the crucial moment, there is no one to tie the victim down—until his father, Ajīgarta, suddenly appears and offers to do the job for another hundred cows. This same eager parent also volunteers to kill the boy, for payment of another hundred. He steps forward, sharpening the knife. Now Śunaḥśepa realizes that he will truly be killed, "as if he were not human" *(amānuṣam iva)*; and he turns to the gods for help, reciting a series of verses from *Ṛgveda* 1.24–30 addressed to Prajāpati, Agni, Savitṛ, Varuṇa, Agni again, the Viśve devāḥ, Indra, the Aśvins, and Uṣas. As he chants these words, the ropes binding him fall away, and at the same time the swollen belly of Hariścandra is finally healed.

Clearly, this boy is gifted with wisdom and vision: the priests ask him to teach them the remaining parts of the ritual. Exhausted, Śunaḥśepa sits down on Viśvāmitra's lap. This is the occasion for a final bitter interchange: after his son's stunning success, the greedy father, Ajīgarta, asks to have him back; but Viśvāmitra refuses, claiming him now as his own son, the god-given Devarāta. The biological father reminds his son of his ancestry and birth, but Śunaḥśepa has been shocked and traumatized: "You chose three hundred cows over me. Everyone saw you holding the knife—something unknown even among the Śūdras." Ajīgarta now offers to buy Śunaḥśepa back, but the boy indignantly refuses: "Someone who has once done an evil thing may well do it again. You have not left your Śūdra ways; your act cannot be healed." And Viśvāmitra adds: "[Ajīgarta] Sauyavasi was truly horrible as he stood with knife in hand, ready to cut. Do not be his son; become my son."

Still, there is a problem, which Śunaḥśepa wants to clear up:

how can he, a Brahmin, an Āṅgirasa, become the son of a Kṣatriya prince *(rājaputra)*, which is what Viśvāmitra is? Viśvāmitra simply restates the proposition: Śunaḥśepa will become his eldest, and the first to inherit. Śunaḥśepa wonders, with reason, if Viśvāmitra's other sons will agree to this; and, indeed, out of these hundred sons, the elder fifty—down to, but not including, the middle son, Madhucchandas—dislike the whole idea. In retaliation for this attitude, their father curses them to inherit the ends of the earth—as the low-caste or outcaste Andhras, Puṇḍras, Śabaras, Pulindas, Mūtibas, etc. The younger fifty—having just heard this chilling curse—accept their father's recommendation and stand behind Śunaḥśepa; as a result, their contented father promises them the wealth of cattle and heroic sons—while their new brother will inherit *them,* and the knowledge that they know. In this way, Śunaḥśepa achieves the best of both worlds, Kṣatriya leadership and divine knowledge *(daive vede)* proper to the Brahmin. This seductive combination, rich in promise, seems beautifully suited to the ritual context in which his story is recited, in the presence of the newly anointed king.

2

Here is a story which, three times over, shows sons as victims of their fathers. First Hariścandra, however reluctantly, is prepared to sacrifice Rohita to Varuṇa, in compliance with the god's repeated demand (and his own initial promise). Then Śunaḥśepa is sold, quite unsentimentally, by *his* father, to serve as substitute victim, and this same greedy father volunteers, for an additional payment, to carry out the execution. Finally, Viśvāmitra curses those of his sons who refuse to accept Śunaḥśepa's new status as eldest among them. The motivations, of course, are different in each case; only the first approximates the *aqedah* pattern of mysterious child sacrifice issuing out of the relation of god to man. The father is given a child only on condition that he give him back almost immediately; he never questions this necessity, but merely tries to buy time, to put off the inevitable. Life—the life of a child—is here a conditional, always precarious miracle, maintained only by desperate bargaining with a deity eager to reclaim his gift. Of the three fathers, Hariścandra is, nonetheless, the most humane, torn as he seems to be between love for his son and his commitment to the god, or to the principle the god embodies and represents. Taken together, these three fathers offer a trenchant expression of the conflictual, indeed murderous aspect of the father-son bond.

And yet the story begins with a strange assertion of identity in this same relationship. Nārada's answer to the king—a kind of hymn to the son, and a definition of this form of being—builds up to the description of procreation as inherently incestuous. The father enters his wife, who thereby becomes his mother; he is born again, renewed, as the child, who is thus little more than a replica of his father. A wife earns her title, *jāyā,* only because her husband is reborn (*jāyate punaḥ*) in her. It is her maternal potential that really matters, that here absorbs or replaces any erotic aspect of this union. Desire, insofar as it exists at all, is incestuous, not in the a priori sense of Freudian mythology, but a posteriori, in the teleological light of every father's infantile rebirth through the wife-turned-mother. Human beings are no different in this respect from animals and birds, who unite with their mothers. Somewhat surprisingly, Nārada ends his statement on this unflattering note. Despite the initial effusions, it hardly seems an overly enthusiastic recommendation for having sons.

There are several striking elements in this passage, which may well offer a key to the story as a whole. As already remarked, the identification it proposes is contextualized by the strong narrative emphasis on paternal aggression. A father is like his son, indeed actually *is* his son, yet he tends to direct sacrificial violence at this same replicated version of himself. In fact, this linkage between self-reproduction and violence is full of meaning. On one level, our story is an essay on substitution: who, or what, can replace which victim at the stake?[3] The chain of substitutes is a long one, culminating in Śunaḥśepa's successful use of the Vedic mantras—another oral mode, this time linguistic rather than ingestive[4]—in place of a human or animal victim; interesting questions of commensurability attach to this series. But on another level, this seems

3. See comments by Doniger (O'Flaherty), prefaced to her translation of the text (1988), 19–20; as remarked earlier, the notion of substitution is a central theme in Vedic religion generally. See Doniger and Smith (1989).

4. See below, chapter 5 section 4.

to be a story about repetition—specifically, the replication of the father's fate and experience in the life of his son, and the unending cycles of sacrificial rebirth and redeath that define that shared fate. This is the universal law that underlies Varuṇa's part in the transaction: the god gives and takes lives; the procreative father produces offspring that reproduce his own self, only after promising to perform the lethal sacrifice; the two poles of life and death, creation and violent destruction, are completely interdependent, and human beings are caught between them. A person lives out his life in the brief respite granted the sacrificial victim (a respite won by the father, who will nevertheless eventually revert to his unhappy role as sacrificer). In this sense, this *aqedah*-like scenario has less to do with the god *per se,* a willful being hungry for the child, than with a divine structure or process built into the world as Vedic man perceives it.

We could restate this double perspective—the issue of substitution in relation to repetition—as reflecting a contrast or tension between two distinct types of reproduction. There is, first, the divine or cosmic law of cyclical, sacrificial regeneration, in which each new birth recapitulates the career of the dying parent; and there is also, perhaps, a more properly human mode of sequential, linear generativity based ultimately on some form of substitution (one victim replaced by another, whose life is then saved by the sacred chant).[5] The latter process, always insecure and dependent upon special forms of knowledge, is contextualized by the overriding power of the former, cosmic law. In this sense, Śunaḥśepa represents an unpredictable, indeed heroic breakthrough. I will return to this point below.

Both Hariścandra and Rohita are trapped inside the cycle of sacrificial origins and conclusions. Neither knows what to do in order to extricate himself from this charmed circle: the father eventually gives in and asks his son to accept the role of victim; the unwilling boy runs away to the wilderness, although guilt draws him back, once a year, to the village. And even the wilderness is no refuge, for all its attributes of potential fertility, dynamism, and supernal sweetness, which Indra stresses in his annual meetings with the runaway. It is not until the wandering Rohita

5. I wish to thank Don Handelman for the insight leading to this distinction.

finds Śunaḥśepa—also, we note, a product of the wilderness—that he, Rohita, is released from the fate his father has prepared for him, while Hariścandra is healed from the illness sent by the god.

All of this illuminates the measure of Śunaḥśepa's achievement. He, and he alone, breaks through the constraining limits of sacrificial causality, operating in its most literal and brutal mode. His father, surely the worst of the three pictured here, perfectly exemplifies the notion of deadly paternal aggression at work within the sacrificial system. Ajīgarta is a monstrous image of the violent father, knife raised above his son's head; but he is clearly part of the same world as Hariścandra, and no less bound by its inner laws. Śunaḥśepa, on the other hand, escapes death at the stake by invoking the gods in Vedic verses. Look at this image: the child singing, as the ropes fall away from his body. Language, the sacred text, the knowledge that it represents—all these, in the right hands, offer a way out of the trap that has held Hariścandra and Rohita captive. Śunaḥśepa has this redeeming knowledge. But the other side of his success is his outright rejection of the now contrite and craven Ajīgarta, who would like to reclaim the prodigy. There is no going back into the nightmare of repetition and replication from which Śunaḥśepa has just escaped. He will not recapitulate his father's career; he moves forward, away from the cyclical violence that consumes the victim, that identifies fathers with their sons. Indeed, Śunaḥśepa actually chooses a new father for himself (Viśvāmitra), although the transition is far from easy and involves yet another act of fierce paternal aggression. But in this respect, too, Śunaḥśepa is the inverse of Hariścandra: the latter wants a son who will, so Nārada has taught him, perpetuate the cycle of birth; Śunaḥśepa seeks a father who will not.

How is it that this child knows the right words, knows how to save himself, find a new way, when everyone else is a helpless prey to the violent processes of repetition? Before we try to answer this question, let us restate what we have learned so far. The text opens with an equation: the father repeats himself in his son; a wife is no different from a mother; reproduction is at once incestuous and cyclical by nature. This perspective is what might be called the biological extension of a sacrificial ideology, whereby birth is always rebirth, and always a step toward (re)death. God gives a child only to demand it back, in a similarly ceaseless cycle. In terms of the father's relation to his son, this double vision seems to require an element of violence. Reproduction, on both the human and the divine levels, is bound up with sacrifice.[6] The text might almost be seeking a way out of this circle—some form of linear progression through the generations, that could allow human life and its emotions a greater measure of autonomy—although the explicit ideology articulated at the onset offers no such hope. Reborn in his son, the father offers up this new version of himself, this substitute self, to the god. The son who is equated with, in effect swallowed up by, his father will die in perpetuating the repetitive cycle. Notice that, in this light, generativity itself has a lethal aspect.

But for this last point, we find ourselves very close to familiar Greek materials. There, too, violence reproduces itself in repetitive cycles through the generations. Think of the house of Atreus: the grandfather, Tantalus, serves his own son, Pelops, to the Olympians, who resurrect the victim when they realize what (or whom) they are supposed to be eating; Pelops, in the next generation, has his own, rather different reasons to be cursed, but his wife, Hippodameia, kills her son or stepson, Chrysippus; her other sons, Atreus and Thyestes, quarrel, and Atreus feeds Thyestes' children to their father in a gruesome feast. All this forms the background to, and overdetermines, the bloody career of Atreus's famous son Agamemnon, who sacrifices his daughter Iphigenia—ostensibly in order to set free the stalled Greek fleet.[7] This sacrifice, too, perpetuates the chain of violence: Agamemnon is slain by his vengeful wife, Clytemnestra, who is then murdered by her son, Orestes.

Throughout this cycle, as in others explored by the tragedians, the killing of children is perhaps the primary focus and motivating theme; as Bennet Simon has shown, in tragedy intrafamilial, intergenerational violence, usually directed against children, almost al-

6. See the formulation by Malamoud (1989, 105): "Le sacrifiant mortel est l'image de l'Homme primordial, dont le dispositif sacrificiel est, de son côté aussi, la reproduction."

7. That Agamemnon's motivations are, in fact, considerably more complex is made plain by both Euripides, throughout *Iphigenia in Aulis,* and Aeschylus (see *Agamemnon* 219–27). This issue deserves further discussion; see also Simon (1988), 49–59.

ways "invites repetition of traumatic sacrifice."[8] This central theme informs a more abstract and general concern with blocked generativity and continuity: the traumatized family, locked into recurrent violence, ultimately destroys its future. Here it is not generativity itself which is imbued with potential violence, as in the Vedic understanding, but an initial act of destruction that spirals inexorably through subsequent generations. The story of Oedipus, which intersects that of the house of Atreus, is another case in point: although the mainstream interpretations tend, wrongly, in my view, to see Oedipus as the victim of a fate articulated by the oracle, one might wonder if his tragic development is not determined to a large degree by the initial act of violence against him, the decision taken by his terrified parents to expose him at birth.

3

Oedipus is close to Śunaḥśepa in another respect, one intimately linked to the question we have asked: how does the child from the wilderness know what he knows? Sophocles' Oedipus is obsessed with knowledge, ultimately, and more precisely, with self-knowledge, especially in relation to horrifying (though unintentional) patricide and incest. The *Brāhmaṇa* tale of Śunaḥśepa has remarkably similar concerns, seen, however, from a radically different perspective. Let us go back for a moment to Nārada's initial statement about sons, with its explicit symbolism of incest. Nārada is answering a question, but his answer seems to contain an underlying question of its own: how is it that a child is both like and different from his parents? That is, the identification of which we have spoken, the father equated with his son, might also be seen as a problem, even a riddle to be solved. Nārada has established a relationship based on the superimposition of one domain (the father or parent) on another (the succeeding generation of children). The repetitive and cyclical effects of this identification, which are real enough in the realm of sacrificial ritual and its metaphysics, need not obscure its inherently paradoxical quality. The fit, in other words, is not quite complete; we are dealing, as so often in the *Brāhmaṇa* texts, with an esoteric, "mystical" correspondence between two normally disparate terms. This is a matter

8. Simon (1988), 24.

of some importance. The entire interchange between Hariścandra and the sage is reminiscent of the "enigma exchanges" *(brahmodya)* which formed an essential part of the Vedic sacrificial cult.[9] An enigmatic question produces oblique and often equally enigmatic responses based on precisely the type of correspondences and identifications *(bandhu)* mentioned above. Above all, the *brahmodya* seeks the conflation or superimposition of distinct domains by establishing an esoteric identity between seemingly disparate items—horse and bird, ocean and sky,[10] father and son.

Nārada's ten verses may not fit the classic *brahmodya* format, but their function is not far removed from this arena. Given the general drive toward conflating levels, it is perhaps not surprising that incest (on the mythic level) is a recurrent topic for the Vedic enigmas;[11] and it is thus natural to find it again here, with reference to the family and reproduction, in a context directly related to the sacrifice. The verses set out the terms of correspondence in a startling and paradoxical set of formulations that, significantly, produce no further response from the listener; it is almost as if Hariścandra were lost within the paradox, whose dangerous framework, straddling the boundary between life and death, also subsumes the life of his son. The sacrifice itself, we should recall, is a means of linking disparate domains, of revealing the hidden connections that make up the unseen texture of reality; within this process, father issues into son, and son into father, through recursive acts of violence. The enigma exchanges, however indirect and obscure they may appear, help to articulate this frame.

There is, however, a difference between being caught up in the enigma and controlling it from a position of knowledge, and the latter is Śunaḥśepa's great gift. Who is this Brahmin boy with the obscene name of "Dog-penis"? He is certainly no ordinary Brahmin, any more than are his brothers, "Dog-ass" and "Dog-tail." The hungry father, Ajīgarta, is also very remote from the Brahminical ideal; Śunaḥśepa scornfully rebukes him for his "Śūdra nature" *(śaudra)*. This family inhabits the wild spaces outside the village, in the domain of wanderers such as the fugitive

9. Note that Hariścandra's question uses the *brahmodya* formula *kiṃ svid:* see Renou (1978), 98. On the *brahmodya,* see Johnson (1980); Shulman (in press b).

10. See examples cited by Renou (1978), 98–105.

11. *RV* 1.71.5; 1.164.33–35; see Renou (1978), 106.

Rohita. Yet Śunaḥśepa himself makes the journey from the wilderness *(araṇya)* to the village *(grāma)*, where Hariścandra's sacrifice is to take place. This intended victim embraces in his own being the intertwined yet polarized categories that constitute the Vedic spatial map. In this sense, he is a kind of prototypical sacrificer, since man *(puruṣa)*, the ultimate sacrificial being, assumes this role precisely because of his double nature, his links with both wilderness and village, like the sacrificial post *(yūpa)* that is carved to his measure.[12] But Śunaḥśepa's encompassing aspect also extends to the social arena; he absorbs in himself not only the wilderness and the settled zone but also the two normally separate categories of Brahmin and Kṣatriya/king, and perhaps, like his father, the two ends of the spectrum, Brahmin and Śūdra, as well.[13]

The conflation of domains that is so central to the enigma is a natural part of Śunaḥśepa's nature. He is, in himself, a walking enigma, a product of the always ambiguous middle space (he is the middle, *madhyama*, son of his parents) which opens up to include the polarized extremes.[14] More precisely, we should place him in the middle of a hierarchical series of related levels of being, and thus capable of encompassing both the primary, cyclical generativity of the cosmos and the sequential reproduction of human beings, dependent on symbolic substitution.[15] This, after all, is his special gift: knowledge grants him egress from the cyclical violence of the sacrifice by affirming the positive potential of substitution. Śunaḥśepa thus also conflates the rival forms of generativity—cosmic and human, cyclical and sequential—that we noticed earlier. Picture him, perhaps, as a wild, weird dog-man, an excluded Brahmin of the wandering Vrātya type, closely connected with impurity and violence, with the play of dice, with a

12. Malamoud (1989), 105–106. See the description of Śunaḥśepa as a "human sacrificial animal" (*puruṣaṃ paśum*), although he objects to being treated "not as a human being" (*amānuṣam iva*).

13. This double identity, as king and Brahmin, is the subject of explicit discussion between Śunaḥśepa and Viśvāmitra (who, incidentally, is himself an exemplar of this conflation, a king who moves across the category boundary to become a Brahmin sage).

14. For a different approach to Śunaḥśepa's "radical middleness" (seen as defined by what it is not, "non-definition, dis-order") see White (1986), 236, 258 and passim. Cf. Weller (1956) and Robinson (1911).

15. I wish to thank Don Handelman again.

certain type of sacrifice—the *sattra* performed by hungry Brahmins, like Śunaḥśepa's father!—and with the esoteric *brahma*-knowledge that accompanies this rite.[16] The Vrātyas are, in fact, sometimes identified as dogs.[17] They are outsiders who nonetheless preserve, or rather enact, the vital and mysterious connections between categorical domains. Śunaḥśepa, as a person of this type, brings to the royal sacrifice this principle of esoteric connectedness embodied in his ambiguous identity, or in the knowledge that it evokes.

Indeed, *being* and *knowing* are somehow equivalent in this context, as in so many areas of Indian thought. Epistemology shades off into ontology, and vice versa: to know the truth is to become that truth, in a transformative and experiential manner. Śunaḥśepa succeeds in overcoming sacrificial death because, as the *Brāhmaṇa* formula repeatedly puts it, "he knows thus," and the one who knows the secret correspondences, the hidden meaning of the sacrifice, no longer dies as a victim of its necessary violence. Śunaḥśepa knows the "answer," if we can use this word, to the enigma, including the *brahmodya*-like exchange about fathers and sons at the opening of our text; he knows the answer to be "himself." He, the human being who uses language to link domains, is one possible solution to the riddle of birth. He is at once his father and himself, earthbound and heaven-oriented, the point of movement and connection between categories, a "unitary understanding"[18] embodied in an identity. The proper answer to the *brahmodya* is not a technical response but an affirmation: "I am" (the earth, the sacrifice, the navel of the cosmos), although it may be couched as "I know" (the navel, the end of the earth).[19]

16. See the detailed study by Falk (1986), 17–72. On hunger and the *sattra:* 30–36, 66; on the *brahmādyam annam,* 44–49. See also Heesterman (1962). Falk points to the links with the *rājasūya,* the ritual context for the Śunaḥśepa story; note that the recitation of this story directly follows on the game of dice in that ritual. See Falk (1986), 164.

17. Ibid., 18–19; and see Sontheimer (1981) and (1989) on the *vāghyā,* the dog-like devotees of Mallāri/Khaṇḍobā in present-day Maharastra. White (1991), 81–84, also recognizes a connection between our story and the Vrātyas.

18. Renou (1978), 104.

19. Ibid. Similarly with Yudhiṣṭhira's successful responses to the Yakṣa's enigmatic questions (*praśna*); the trial ends with Yudhiṣṭhira's request to be exactly as he already is (though successfully hidden). See Shulman (in press b). We note in

The point, in cases like this, is not to straighten out the confusing superimpositions and category-fusions inherent in the genre, but rather to live them out, to embody them in a knowing, dynamic presence. In this respect, the Vedic enigma differs markedly from the classical riddle, with its disambiguating drive.

Think, again, of Oedipus, solver of riddles. As Vernant has shown in a penetrating essay, Oedipus is, simultaneously and paradoxically, the living answer to the riddle of the Sphinx—he is at one and the same time child, father, and brother, i.e., the four-footed, three-footed, and two-footed being who is "man." Normally, these identities are sequential, but Oedipus collapses them into a single stage, when he is husband and child to his wife, father and brother to his children; he is a man who "as he advances in age jumbles up and confuses the social and cosmic order of the generations instead of respecting it."[20] The incestuous doubling of roles that the Śunaḥśepa text sees as normative to the father-son relation is, for Oedipus, a tragically literal truth realized in the retrograde, cyclical movement of his evolving (actually devolving) career. He fails, of course, to see that he is the real subject of the riddle, and Sophocles' text accordingly centers on the process of his gaining an understanding that can only be a source of dread.

The underlying hope, for the Greek audience, is that this horror-filled conflation of roles can somehow be disentangled, the retrograde movement reversed, and a lucid rearticulation of categories made possible; Oedipus, the conflated being, becomes a scapegoat to this process. Śunaḥśepa, by way of contrast, knows and accepts his paradoxical double nature. Indeed, it is precisely this knowledge that sets him free. Where Oedipus demonstrates the curse of mixing sequential roles, Śunaḥśepa brings with him the blessing of conflation and connectedness. He knows and is the sacrifice that activates unseen connections; and, in the Vedic system, it is precisely this form of reflexive consciousness that, by internalizing the entire process in the knowing self, permits transcendence of its inherent evil and violence. We begin to see why the author of our

---

passing that such statements of identity are frequently the culminating answer to a series of riddles, especially of the "neck-riddle" type, where one's life hangs in the balance; see, for example, Puccini's *Turandot*.

20. Vernant (1982), 25.

text assures us that reciting it frees one from evil. Note that the comparison we have been pursuing also corresponds to more general cosmological or axiological concerns: Greek sacrifice, it has been said, aims at disambiguating and separating categorical domains;[21] Vedic sacrifice is a form of connecting them, of bringing the sacrificer into heaven as a (temporarily) divine being, a divinized trans-form of the normative self.

Following the direction of interpretation that emerged from our discussion of the Ciṟuttŏṇṭar-Siriyāla materials, we might read the Śunaḥśepa story as embodying a characteristic process of psychometaphysical growth, a process in some ways radically different from that described in the Tamil and Telugu texts. There, as we saw, the movement tends toward the literal, the infra-symbolic; no substitute victim is allowed, and there is no escape from the entire emotional experience of sacrifice at its most brutal and raw. Ciṟuttŏṇṭar, like King Maṉunītikaṇṭacoḻaṉ, is driven to a place free from symbolism, even beyond language, where painful emotion exists in its paradoxical fullness and power. Śunaḥśepa, however, saves himself through the full internalization of the symbolic—it is the failure of Hariścandra and Rohita to achieve this possibility that condemns them to cyclical, horrific violence—in a movement within consciousness that then acts upon the world. This is the level at which paradox enters the Vedic system, through the symbolic identification of disparate entities, which both are and are not literally united; Śunaḥśepa is and is not his father; the conflation is real, rich in meaning, yet not exhausted by the literal. Paradox, quite properly situated, like Śunaḥśepa himself, in the middle zone between distinct poles or vectors, transforms awareness, with the inevitable concomitant transformation in being. We thus have three primary stages: symbolic connection, paradoxical identification, and transformation leading to the "victim's" escape from sacrifical dying. This process may well be considered paradigmatic for this type of sacrifice.[22]

21. Vernant (1988), 183–201.

22. Hence, perhaps, Śunaḥśepa's role as exemplar, and the story's prominence in the ritual in which it is embedded. It would seem, however, that the conflation of Brahmin and Kṣatriya identities in the story is also central to this point in the *rāja-sūya,* where the king's role in relation to the Brahmins is being articulated.

We are still, with Śunaḥśepa, some distance away from the Upaniṣadic model of esoteric initiation, often of the son by his violent father, as we will see in the next chapter. But our story already points, at least, in this direction: Śunaḥśepa's ordeal involves the living through of self-transforming knowledge gained after rejection—in fact, a violent attack—by the father, whom the son is meant to surpass. The father's rejection thus becomes, in effect, his truest gift to his son. Knowledge, and survival, proceed from this difficult point. And the gods, at the very least, abet this process of learning truth through undergoing the sacrifice. Hariścandra and Rohita stop, too soon, because of natural attachment and dread of loss; in the language of our texts, they never reach "the end of the sacrifice." But the basic principle, at work in the enigmatic mingling of worlds and in the interpenetration of life and death, remains imbued with mystery and transformative power. The real secret, which Śunaḥśepa intuitively acts out, lies in assimilating the enigma to the self—thus making oneself the elusive link to invisible and otherwise disconnected levels of the real.

4

Later versions of the story revise the contours of the family drama, thereby altering its meaning. In the *Bālakāṇḍa* of the *Rāmāyaṇa,* Śunaḥśepa is no longer a heroic figure, who seeks the answers to the riddles of birth and sacrifice in himself; rather, he is simply the beneficiary of his maternal uncle *(mātula)* Viśvāmitra's helpful teaching and advice. Hariścandra and Rohita have disappeared from the story; the sacrificing king is Ambarīṣa of Ayodhyā, who has the misfortune to have his intended animal-victim stolen by Indra. (The epic and *purāṇic* Indra, as we know, tends to regard successful human sacrificers as threatening rivals.) Looking for an alternative victim, preferably human, the king finds the sage Ṛcīka on Bhṛgutunda Mountain; Ambarīṣa offers to buy one of the sage's sons. Once again, the father refuses to part with his eldest, and the mother holds fast to the youngest; now the middle son, Śunaḥśepa, perceiving his position vis-à-vis his parents and brothers only too clearly and tragically, volunteers to go with the king: "It looks as if the middle son is already sold—so take me away" (*vikrītaṃ madhyamaṃ manye rājan putraṃ nayasva mām,* 1.61.21). The father gets a thousand cows and other riches, and Śunaḥśepa mounts the king's chariot.

But on the way to the sacrificial site, while resting at the sacred site of Puṣkara, they encounter Viśvāmitra, whom Śunaḥśepa immediately recognizes as his uncle. The desperate boy pleads with the latter to save him, since no one else can help, "I have no father or mother, nor other relatives. . . . Save me, as a father would his son." This last, perhaps ironic statement, given Śunaḥśepa's recent experience, immediately wins the uncle over; Viśvāmitra now turns to his own surviving sons[23] with an extreme demand. "The time has arrived to achieve that goal—the goodness of the other world (*paralokahitārtha*)—that is the real reason fathers produce sons. This young boy has sought refuge with me; do what is right for his sake, even at the cost of your lives. Become victims at the rite, and give satisfaction to Agni—so that Śunaḥśepa will have a protector, the sacrifice will be unimpeded, the gods satisfied, and my promise kept." Here is a new and radical formulation of the unending riddle of procreation: if in the *Brāhmaṇa* text the father regenerates himself in his son, here he produces life for the sake of a metaphysical goal—his future welfare in the other world. This statement, even if it arises from the unstable and often misguided consciousness of Viśvāmitra, deserves to be taken seriously, as we will see in the next chapter. In any case, the sons reject it with scorn: how can their father save someone else's son at the cost of *their* lives? It is like eating dog's flesh; they will have no part of this exchange. The result, as in the *Brāhmaṇa* text, is that their irascible and disappointed father curses them to become outcastes, eaters of dog-meat, for a thousand years.

Now that the aggression against the son is fully achieved, on both sides—Ṛcīka's avaricious sale of Śunaḥśepa, and Viśvāmitra's curse against his sons—the devoted uncle can teach his nephew two verses *(gāthā)* to be chanted at the stake. Thus provided, Śunaḥśepa eagerly urges the king to the sacrifice. Tied to the sacrificial post, the boy chants the verses in honor of Indra and Upendra; Indra, pleased, gives the boy the promise of a long life,

23. One hundred of his sons have already been slaughtered in Viśvāmitra's unsuccessful battle with his perennial rival, Vasiṣṭha.

while Ambarīṣa happily reaches the end of the sacrifice *(yajña-syāntam)* after all.[24]

As in the *Brāhmaṇa* version, the middle son's predicament is basic to this version; but the real point of Śunaḥśepa's middle position—his ability to recognize and embody the esoteric connections—has been lost, and, instead, family dynamics have come to dominate the story.[25] The maternal uncle turns out to be more compassionate, more "paternal," toward his nephew than the latter's natural father—though this same uncle acts in rage against his own sons. From the son's point of view, it is clearly the father who is most dangerous—often, it seems, because of some conscious metaphysical or ethical stand. Śunaḥśepa's escape now assumes almost a technical character, the near-automatic result of manipulating the proper *mantras;* in essence, this is no longer his story, but that of Viśvāmitra's costly triumph. The Kṣatriya determined to become a Brahmin is able to demonstrate something of his new-found power, though not without striking out at his own sons; this Brahmin-to-be has not yet conquered anger. As to the issue of knowledge, so crucial to the earlier text, it appears that here Śunaḥśepa's only real gain is the perhaps unwelcome insight into his father's attitude and nature; thus in Kampaṉ's Tamil version of this episode, at the moment of decision, when each of his parents chooses one of his brothers, Śunaḥśepa is said to turn away from them with a laugh, the bitter signal of new-found understanding.[26] We may remember Śiva's smile when he comes down, hungry to the point of murder, to the village of the Little Devotee.[27]

Some *purāṇic* versions of this story follow the *Rāmāyaṇa*'s presentation relatively closely.[28] Others, however, somewhat surprisingly, revert to the pattern of the *Aitareya Brāhmaṇa,* our first text. In *Devībhāgavatapurāṇa,* Hariścandra prays to Varuṇa for a son,

24. *Rām.* 1. 61–62.

25. The same concern with the vulnerability of the middle child is worked out prominently in Bhāsa's *Madhyamavyāyoga.*

26. *Irāmāvatāram* of Kampaṉ 1.675: *maṟṟaiya maintaṉ nākku.*

27. The full-throated laughter of the child about to be sacrificed by his parents also provides the enigmatic climax to the cynical story of filicide in *Vetālapañca-viṃśatikā* 20.

28. Thus *Bhāgavatapurāṇa* 9.7; *Brahmāṇḍapurāṇa* 2.3.66.66–68.

and it is the god who first broaches the notion of sacrifice—the condition of fulfilling the king's request. Here the old notion of cyclical and lethal generativity is firmly rooted in the god's demands upon his worshipers.[29] Hariścandra succeeds in repeatedly putting off the sacrifice, as in the *Brāhmaṇa* account, until the moment arrives when the boy has to escape to the forest to save himself. When, hearing of his father's illness, he returns to the village, Indra appears to teach him that "the self *(ātman)* is dear to all living beings; only for the sake of one's own self are sons, wives, and riches dear." It is thus hardly surprising that the boy's father is prepared to sacrifice him, to save his own body (7.16.7)! We have come some ways from Nārada's original teaching, to the effect that the son *is* the father's self, incestuously reproduced; but the latter theme is resumed, in a negative form, when Ajīgarta draws near to slay *his* son, the bound and screaming Śunaḥśepa. This vision is unbearable for all who are present at the sacrifice—priests, royal counselors, and other spectators; they cry out in pain, denounce Ajīgarta as a criminal, cannibalistic demon *(piśāca)* in Brahmin form. "The son is born out of the body as one's own self *(ātman);* so the Vedas say. How then can you, in your evil mind, seek to kill your own self?" (7.16.36–37). The essential, if problematic equation of father and son, what we have identified as the underlying riddle posed by this story, thus survives into the *purāṇic* retelling.

This same riddle is reformulated by our hero, Śunaḥśepa, after his successful escape from death. "Whose son am I now?" he asks the assembled Brahmins, and a lively debate develops: some assert that he cannot renounce his birth, and the biological father who reared him; others are in favor of declaring the king, who purchased him, his father—or perhaps it is Varuṇa, who freed him from his fetters, who deserves the title. Vasiṣṭha ultimately decides the dispute in favor of Viśvāmitra, who taught the boy the *mantra* that made the god appear. Given the sequence of aggressive acts aimed at this child, we can by now easily understand how paternity itself can be called in question. It is almost as if Śunaḥśepa could, and indeed should, do entirely without a father of any kind; having one is just too dangerous a business for any child. Never-

29. Similarly, *Brahmapurāṇa* 104.20.

theless, we note that Śunaḥśepa himself poses the question, and seems to need an answer; the father he finally "adopts" is, in fact, his teacher, a striking (but probably vain) attempt to displace the tensions inherent to the original father-son relation onto an all too similar figure.[30]

Rather than pursuing the further permutations of this story in *purāṇa* and *kāvya,* let me attempt to restate this last theme, which may well constitute its core. A vector of destructiveness runs through the relations of fathers and sons, from the child's birth (or even before it) to the culminating achievement of self-knowledge. Every person is a riddle—a little himself, a little his parents and siblings—to be "solved," so to speak, in the Vedic context, by sacrifice. But in this case the solution is not meant to dissolve the initial mystery. Riddles first conflate, then disambiguate distinct levels or domains; but the sacrifice enacted by Śunaḥśepa articulates the paradox of the child's double identity in an enigma-like equation, which works on the consciousness of the intended victim. Śunaḥśepa experiences the unresolved paradoxes of reproduction, both the peculiar amalgam of self and other in the child, and the dynamic of obsolescence that operates within this relation. A father, to be truly a father, will ultimately disappear into his son. Fathers, like teachers, are meant to be replaced. The significant feature is that this perception is brought home to the boy-hero only when he is tied to the sacrificial stake.

Notice, again, the distinction between Rohita and Śunaḥśepa. The former remains wholly bound up in the murderous cycle of determining paternal identity: indeed, neither Rohita nor Hariścandra can free himself from this nightmarish equation, in which the gift of life comes at the cost of that same life. Śunaḥśepa, by way of contrast, is completely cut off by his monstrous father, and thus cast on his own resources; he finds within himself, by himself, the redemptive words of appeal to the gods. Aggression by the parent thus takes two separate forms in this story: there is the inherent destructiveness of biological generativity, which reproduces

30. Similarly, *Brahmapurāṇa* 104.83–85. It is noteworthy that the *Devībhāgavata* establishes a direct linkage between the Śunaḥśepa story, as summarized above, and the *purāṇic* accounts of Hariścandra's terrible testing (initiated by Viśvāmitra). A version of the Hariścandra story follows the conclusion of Śunaḥśepa's tale, when Vasiṣṭha defends his protegé Hariścandra in the face of Viśvāmitra's scathing attacks.

the parent in the child; and there is the extreme form of brutal rejection by the parent that can become the ground for autonomy and insight. The latter case may be coded either as sacrifice or as gnosis, but it is always linked to a metaphysical stance. In our story, we find the intuition of ultimacy as situated (or as accessible) at the place of binding, the stake connecting this world and the next through a ritual act of violence. In the sacrificial context generally, this vision of the stake is the knowledge offered by father to son; so overpowering is this knowledge that the gift often appears as a form of filicide.

Stated differently, there is a reduplicated and complementary relation to death that fits our distinction between two forms of aggression. The father can only reconstitute himself in his child by partly dying himself, or by killing: this is the condition on which the god grants the child in the first place. For his part, the child, to become the father that he must someday be, disappears into *his* father's experience, dying or almost dying at the latter's command. In the case of Śunaḥśepa, this experience of the ultimate, in its destructive aspect, takes the dark form of attempted child-sacrifice.

But here language redeems, knowledge can save, the symbol redefines the terms of what is true: the child *becomes* the set of symbolic equations, a walking metaphor, the living point of connectiveness and hence of transformation. Such a center subsumes violence and evil; whoever tells this story, undergoing its process, is therefore free. In effect, one identifies oneself with a total cosmic system motivated by fundamental forces of violent negation; these forces can be transcended only by such identification with the whole that contains them. Somewhat surprisingly, this process, which we have stated in abstract terms, is firmly entrenched within the family, with its given structures of intergenerational conflict. There is a certain boldness about the way our authors present this insight. For them, the father's attack upon the child—already implicit, it would appear, in the very moment of conception—is, on the one hand, the inevitable reflection of a cosmic condition that links creativity with destruction, and identity with familiar and substantial forms of self-alienation; on the other hand, this attack, if sustained to the point of breakthrough, can become the necessary precondition of liberating knowledge.

5

On Teaching the Truth: Vyāsa Loses Śuka

«мир лишь луч от лика друга, все иное—
тень его!»

The world is but a ray
from the face of a friend,
and all the rest—his shadow.
—Gumilyov

1

Father and son sit together at the top of the world. Except for the birds, the rocks, the trees, and the flowing water, they are quite alone. (Occasionally a radiant woman, a bird-like *apsaras,* may fly past overhead.) The others have left the mountain: brilliant Jaimini, and Paila, and Sumantu, and Vaiśampāyana, who can never forget. These four pupils of the father asked to return to the world, and Vyāsa let them go. He sat and watched them begin their long descent. They will carry his voice, his teaching, everywhere, as teachers of Veda: through them, the sacred words will continue to sound from the throats of men.

And now the mountain is silent but for the birdsong, the murmur of water. Father and son sit together, alone. Bereft of his pupils, the father no longer has the heart to recite the sacred texts. Nor does the son wish to be taught. They have nothing more to say to one another.

Vivid images from the past attend their silence. Here, on this mountain, the god Viṣṇu tortured himself to obtain a son; here Pārvatī, the mountain's stony daughter, was given to Śiva as a bride; here the young hero Skanda, fruit of that incongruous union, boasted of his prowess and brandished his great spear. These memories inform the consciousness of the two silent men, who are preparing for another, equally memorable deed.

The silence is pregnant with feeling. On one side, there is impatience mingled with suspicion: Why is he holding me back? Why did he insist on my joining the Vedic recitation, the *adhyayana,* before the others left? Has he forgotten what he himself taught me? Beneath these questions there lurks, perhaps, a deeper and still angrier thought. On the other side, the father is feeling the unexpected flooding of anxiety (how many hitherto unknown emotions has this strange son brought into his father's life?). Both know that this is the silence of impending separation. The father refuses to understand, and neither of the two will utter the first word.

In such silence, truth abides, though it can hardly endure: soon Nārada, the wandering sage, will arrive to protest the sudden absence on this holy mountain of the *brahmaghoṣa,* the Vedic chant, the noise of God. The ears of this meddlesome traveler ache from the quiet. Why is Vyāsa no longer teaching his son? He, Nārada, must insist. Holy sounds should issue from a sacred spot, thereby dispelling the perennially threatening darkness *(tamas).* Reluctantly—for how much will break and shatter at the first tone, at this intimate juncture?—father and son take up the chant once more. But not for long. Suddenly, a violent wind blows over the mountain top, and Vyāsa stops to teach of the essence of wind, which precedes and activates the human voice. There are, he tells Śuka, many kinds of wind, which is breath, which is life itself, which, at bottom, is but the rhythmic exhalation of God. There is much to learn of this subject, rich, exfoliated typologies, a wealth of unexpected connections: Vyāsa warms to the exposition. The words that carry exact and true knowledge, that classify and record and capture the real in its subtlety and obscurity, these words are flowing again, another, final gift of the father to his son. There is even a practical conclusion: "because of all that I am telling you, those who know God *(brahman)* do not recite when a great wind is blowing, for God might be hurt by this *(brahma tat pīḍitaṃ bhavet).* Therefore, stop your recitation now."

And without further speech, the father goes off to bathe in the heavenly river, Gaṅgā, leaving his son alone with Nārada.

The father's heart is unaccountably heavy. Was it wrong to become a father? Pupils are easier: they internalize, to a greater or lesser degree, what you want to teach them, perhaps even allowing the contradictions and hesitations to survive—although in the end these students, too, go away. Now there is only this boy, who believes, all too literally, what I have said. Everyone can see he is a kind of fool.

Something is wrong, and Vyāsa knows it, remembering how it all began. He had wanted a son, so there was desire. But ascetics like Vyāsa should be free of desire. So, as is customary in this profession, Vyāsa worked upon his desire through the medium of Yoga and austerities, torturing his body. When, at length, Śiva appeared and offered him a boon, Vyāsa said: I want a son equal in manly vigor *(vīrya)* to fire, earth, water, wind, and air. Śiva agreed: "You will have a son pure as fire, wind, earth, water, and air."

Now Vyāsa took hold of the two fire-sticks *(araṇī)* and began rubbing them together. Suddenly, an apparition: the stately Ghṛtācī, a woman beautiful beyond imagining, stood before him. His mind, of course, was overcome with passion and confusion. Noticing this, Ghṛtācī became a parrot *(śukī)* and flew away, her task accomplished, but Vyāsa was lost to himself and the world. His seed fell from him onto the firesticks, which, in his frenzy, he continued to rub together. Thus, out of the firesticks, was born his son, blazing like fire. He was called Śuka, after his entirely absent mother, the *śukī,* and Āraṇeya, because of the *araṇī.* Gaṅgā herself came to wash away the impurities of birth; an antelope's skin and the ascetic's staff, *daṇḍa,* fell from the skies for him, for everyone knew that he was already a chaste and wise ascetic. Śiva, together with the goddess, performed his thread ceremony; Indra offered him a water pot and radiant garments; many birds—geese, cranes, parrots, peacocks, and jays—circled him, joyously screeching out their cries. He was always close to the birds. No sooner was he born than the Vedas, with all their secret parts *(rahasyas),* entered into him, as they had into his father, long ago.

Vyāsa sent his son to study with Bṛhaspati, an expert in the Vedic sciences and their commentaries; and thus Śuka received his early training in the tradition *(itihāsa)* and the learned disciplines *(śāstra)*. When he returned to his father, he was already, in a sense, fully formed. He had no interest in the normal progress of the Brahmin student through the early stages of life, from *brahmacārin* to householder to the *vānaprastha,* who wanders in the forest. Śuka thought only of release—*mokṣa,* the culmination of the human processes of maturation, the Brahmin's last, most distant goal.

And this is what he asked his father: "You are proficient in the subject of *mokṣa;* teach it to me, so that I may find peace of mind *(manasaś śāntiḥ paramā)*." How many boys, how many students, would even formulate such a request? How many would let their thoughts dwell on release, at a moment when life had barely started coursing through their bodies, in the springtime of their powers? Yet Śuka, still a child, was driven to seek peace of mind. What strange power, what consciousness of suffering within him, moved the child in this direction? Vyāsa would always remember his son's unsettling demand, and his own ambiguous reply: "Study *mokṣa* as well as the various forms of dharma." For Vyāsa knew: everything that was to follow lay enfolded, half-articulate, in this critical exchange.

At Vyāsa's command, Śuka devoted himself to the study of Yoga and *Sāṅkhya (kāpilam)*. Seeing his readiness, Vyāsa sent him for further instruction to Janaka, the wise king of Videha, a teacher adept in the hidden truth and in the matter of *mokṣa*. Given his son's steadily accumulating powers, Vyāsa found it necessary to forbid him to go to Videha by flying through the air; Śuka was to walk to Videha, by the ordinary human route. This Śuka did, seeing but not seeing the bountiful landscapes through which he passed, for he was concentrated in himself, delighting in the Self. In Mithilā, Janaka's capital, the gatekeepers at first refused to allow him entry to the palace, until one of them, filled with sorrow *(śoka)*—a sorrow resonating with Śuka's very name—observing him blazing with splendor like the sun itself, took pity and opened the doors. Once inside, he was warmly and regally welcomed, fed, and honored, and Janaka agreed to teach him.

Śuka began by questioning him on the central issue of his young life: "What should a Brahmin do, and what is the nature of release? How is release to be achieved—by knowledge or by austerities?" Janaka's initial response followed the traditional programme sanctioned by the teaching: first, said the king, the Brahmin should complete his course of study; then he should marry and have children and grandchildren, before eventually retiring to the forest; at the end of his life, he can reach the ultimate truth. This statement, of course, could hardly fail to provoke the

God-starved boy. "But is it really necessary," asked Śuka, "to go through all the earlier stages of life, if knowledge already clearly exists in the heart?" Now Janaka, perceiving the nature of this precocious pupil, could indeed offer the shortcut, the reassurance, that Śuka longed for: it *is* possible—if one's senses have been purified through many earlier births—for a person to attain release even in the first stage of his training, as a *brahmacārin*. He must see himself in all beings, and all beings in himself; then, flying away like a bird, leaving his body behind, he becomes free, without duality, extinguished. Moreover, you, Śuka—this is Janaka's intuitive conclusion—have great knowledge and power, although you do not know this; it is only because you are still a child, or because of some doubt or the residual drive of continued existence, that you have not yet gone upon the highest path. One like you, with pure intent, who has cut away doubt and untied the knots of the heart, can reach the end of the way.

There is no ambiguity in this answer; Janaka speaks with certain knowledge, rooted in his own truth. It is with this teaching that Śuka has returned to his father's mountain, to confront Vyāsa one last time, and to take his leave.

Now Vyāsa has gone away to bathe, leaving Śuka alone with Nārada. The mountain echoes with birdcalls, the ripple of streams, and the boy's own silent yearning. Liberated, for the moment, from his father's constraining presence, Śuka brings to the visiting sage his perennial concern, his hope for yet another confirmation: "Please," he says, "connect me (*yoktum arhasi,* the verb of Yoga) with whatever good there may be in this world." Nārada, taking advantage of Vyāsa's absence, can now embark on Śuka's final instruction. This is the last dose of verbal teaching that the boy will ever receive, and it does no more than restate what Śuka already knows—from his father, from Janaka, and from his own congenital instincts.

Nārada begins by quoting Sanatkumāra, who studied with God: there is no eye equal to wisdom, no form of austerities equal to the truth, no evil like passion, no joy like that of renunciation. Nārada then speaks of the happiness that derives from being without ties, and of the misery that is bound up with connectedness. The highest dharma is noninjury *(ānṛśaṃsya)*, the greatest power that of patience and forbearance, the highest knowledge that of the Self—and nothing is higher than truth. Like fish caught in the fisherman's net and hauled, gasping, onto dry land, all living beings writhe in suffering, trapped in the net of affection *(sneha)*. Like a silkworm, one weaves a prison around oneself with the threads of confusion, produced from one's own self; grasping attachment *(parigraha)* to things is at the root of this process. Why walk alone this unmarked path of darkness through the wilderness? When you set out, no one will follow you from behind—except your own good and evil deeds. One should cast off this impermanent, defiled body, held together only by bones and sinews, smeared with blood, foul-smelling, full of feces and urine, a prey to old age and anger and desire. The man tormented by his many deeds ends up by killing other creatures in his desperate attempts to escape his own suffering. Even in pleasure, one is worn away by the inherent deceitfulness of the world, and by the constant willingness to harm others.

This is man's natural offense: the seed produced in one place goes elsewhere; becomes a fetus through attachment to the female sexual organ; is born as a son, with a ghostlike existence, even for those who recoil from the womb as from an angry snake. How does the child manage to survive those disastrous months in the mother's belly, where food and drink are digested and wastes are stored, while the infant's native beauty and its very breath are burned away? Even those who escape this prisonous womb alive eventually join with others to create new offspring, and thus ever more destruction, in that they, too, are helplessly submerged in duality. They are consumed by disease, in constant pain, prepared to pay anything to the doctors to be healed—but these same doctors, for all their herbs and potions, are themselves attacked by illness, as animals are destroyed by hunters. Those select few who survive in relative health are finished off by old age. No one can help this world, which is being swept along in the fierce currents of its own grief and confusion; its basic contours will never change. Everyone tries his best to stay on top of it, but this never succeeds. Don't allow yourself to be seduced: abandon both dharma and *adharma,* abandon both truth and untruth; and when you have gone beyond both truth and untruth, let go of that by which you let them go.

This final phrase, *yena tyajasi tat tyaja,* is the ultimate Hindu teaching on renunciation, and thus the perfect conclusion to Nārada's speech. It is best, of course, to renounce the world, and all binding human ties, but even that is not enough; in the end, to attain release, one must renounce even renunciation itself, lest one remain bound and subjugated by the very fascination of this goal. This is a teaching of direct relevance to the restless Brahmin boy. It is subtly ironic in part: Yoga, the art of "yoking" and "binding," becomes the compelling ideology for the impending disjunction of son from father, who is already painfully "dis-yoked" *(viyukta)* from his beloved students. Moreover, there is some reason to suspect the motives of this meddlesome, gossipy sage, whose words so often work insidiously against the interests and better judgment of his interlocutors. There is something calculated, not wholly innocent, about the images Nārada chooses—the lonely path, where no one ever follows you, except for your own good or evil deeds.

Yet Śuka is confirmed in his decision, which he can now express openly: there is much suffering in having a wife and children, and much toil in reciting the Veda; the only way to freedom from misery is the supreme path of Yoga, by which one renounces his body and, becoming wind, enters the sun. He, Śuka, will dwell there, in the sun, after entering into the mountains, the clouds, the earth, the ten directions of space, and all living beings, from gods to demons. He knows what he must do.

It is time for him to seek out his father. Vyāsa, however, begs him to put off the final departure. "Please, my son, stay one more day, that I may feast my eyes on you." But Śuka is beyond such requests, even beyond love or affection *(nissneha),* and he makes no further reply. The real farewell is wholly embedded, again, in silence.

Śuka leaves. On Mount Kailāsa, in some deserted spot—yet still visible, we are told, to his father—he follows the yogic regimen of withdrawal into the self. Facing east at sunrise, in a yogic posture, in utter silence—no birds fly overhead, there is no sound to be heard—he sees within him his true self, released from all ties. And he laughs, shattering the silence. He has reached his goal.

He can fly—always birdlike, Śuka soars through the skies at will. First he bows to Nārada, to thank him for the gift of Yoga. Then he is on his way, still eastward, toward the sun. He fills the world with sound—not the words of human language, but a purer sound *(śabda),* the song of this flying bird-man on his way to release. He is like a god: this is the conclusion of the beautiful women of heaven, who see him approaching. But one of them, Urvaśī, is troubled: "Soon he will pervade the universe. Yet this son, filled with compassion for his father, has achieved this state *(siddhi)* through obedience to his father. He is firmly devoted to his father *(pitṛbhakta);* how could his father let him go?"

Śuka hears her question. Although he does not respond directly, something has been touched within him. Now, surveying the world—the skies, the earth, mountain and forests, lakes and rivers—he addresses all that he sees: "If my father comes in my wake, crying out my name, all of you must respond to him, out of love for me." And so they promise: the rivers, the four cardinal directions, the oceans and mountains, all take it upon themselves to give this response.

Like a smokeless fire, Śuka stands firm in God, that is devoid of attributes or distinguishing signs *(pade nitye nirguṇe liṅgavarjite brahmani).* Two mountain peaks, one gold and the other silver, appear in his path: he flies directly at them, northwards, and they split in two to allow him through. Now he is over the heavenly Gaṅgā, where the *apsaras*-women are playing their water games. Though they are naked, Śuka's appearance causes them no dismay, for he no longer has any form *(nirākāra),* he is beyond the differentiation of males and females. Indeed, he has already turned into the world, becoming all *(sarvabhūta);* he is now, himself, the mountains and trees and rivers, the earth and the sky. He has disappeared.

The father follows, his heart aching. He sees the split mountain peaks and knows this to be his son's work *(karma).* He calls out, mournfully, as if reciting Veda *(śaikṣeṇa):* "Śukaaa . . ." Nor is he left without an answer, for Śuka, who is everywhere, who has become all, who is the self of all things, who faces everywhere, answers with the single syllable *bhoḥ*—a simple vocative O!, or perhaps an exclamation of sorrow[1]—that echoes through the mountain caverns. The whole world cries out this response. Since then, echoes resound through the mountains for Śuka's sake.

1. See Monier-Williams (1899), s.v.

But Śuka is gone. All qualities and forms, beginning with sound *(śabda)*, he has abandoned forever. He has gone to the highest place. His father knows, and he weeps, thinking only of his lost son. Grief-stricken, unable to free himself from this burden, despite all his years of study and teaching, he wanders to the banks of the Gaṅgā. The women are still there, and this time, as the father approaches, they are desperately ashamed. Some dive into the water to hide their nakedness, some rush for their clothes, some hide in the bushes. The son was free, the father who sired him and taught him is still bound. He knows this, too, knows how his son has surpassed him in everything. He is both happy and ashamed.

Only Śiva can comfort him, the god who first fulfilled the father's bold request. "You asked for a son equal to fire, earth, water, wind, and sky," Śiva says, "and that is the kind of son you got, through your own ascetic power. Now he has reached the highest way, that is difficult for anyone to attain, even for the gods. Why, then, are you grieving? As long as the mountains stand, as long as the oceans exist, your imperishable fame, and that of your son, will endure. And wherever you look, you will always see beside you, never departing, a reflected image (or shadow, *chāyā*) of your son."

Vyāsa looks: the shadow is there. It will always be there. Joyfully, he turns away.[2]

2

Make no mistake. The father has lost his son. His last plea, that Śuka linger one more day, is never even answered in language. Vyāsa's last words to his son are an open question, tenuous, uncertain, revealing the father's weakness. After this, there is only the cry of a name, which comes back at the caller. Śuka has truly gone.

The father is left with three unsatisfactory substitutes—an echo (of his own voice; but it is the world that speaks); a shadow or reflection, visible only to his eyes; and the assurance of the god that the story will survive at least as long as there are mountains and seas. Notice that the story is born out of loss, for which it partly compensates. This father's grief may fade, although other fathers will reexperience it; the story, that speaks of how this fa-

2. *Mahābhārata* (Southern Recension), 12.309–20.

ther taught and parted from his son, remains the best of the god's gifts. The story is itself an echo or a shadow of some more hidden truth, the linguistic reembodiments of which are surely open to doubt. Still, this is what we have.

We will try to address this shadow of a story—minimally, gently, hoping not to injure it, as the wise refrain from reciting Veda into the wind so as not to injure God. Our discussion will focus on three issues: first, the nature of the loss, and its meaning in the context of the epic and the cultural ideals articulated there; second, the relationship of father and son; finally, the implicit metaphysics of this story, including its vision of self in relation to the world (and of language in relation to the world). We conclude with a comparative note on Narcissus and Echo.

We begin by stressing yet again that this is a tale about loss. It is, in fact, the most trenchant narrative expression in the Hindu tradition of the actual emotional price inherent in the cultural ideals of renunciation and release. From the time of the Upaniṣads on, we hear much of the joyful goal of *mokṣa* that, if one is lucky and determined, may follow upon the internal movement away from the world. One renounces the constituents of one's empirical identity—name, family, passions, sensory knowledge, all human ties—in the interests of achieving ultimacy, which is negatively defined; it is "not this" and "not this." The act of negation conduces toward freedom. One should always recall in this context that freedom of this ultimate type is generally perceived, even explicitly characterized, as a joyful fullness of being, a plenum into which the miseries of individuated and egoistical existence have been absorbed. The "negative" state of release is rich in ontic power and, for this very reason, offers surpassing happiness (if one can use such a pale term for so rich a form of being). One empties oneself into the delicious wholeness of one's Self.

Nevertheless, as is well known, the goals of renunciation and release were the object of extreme ambivalence within the mature Hindu tradition; in classical times, as now, yogis and *sannyāsins* frequently aroused suspicion, hostility, or contempt. For that side of the tradition focused on dharma—the accomplishing of one's duties within the fabric of this life—renunciation constituted a real, potentially subversive threat (hence the attempts to defuse its power by mediating schemes such as the graduated progression of *āśrama*-states, from student through householder to forest dweller and renouncer; this is precisely the scheme that Śuka rejects). One could easily document this attitude in detail, and we would do well to remember that the *Mahābhārata,* which provides the context for the story of Śuka, articulates this same ambivalence in a variety of trenchant ways. But, for our purposes, this is not the central point. This story shows us something rather different, i.e., the powerful dimension of loss that accompanies renunciation even under conditions of relatively unambiguous adherence to this ideal. Vyāsa is himself a great yogi, and a *sannyāsin,* who teaches his son—among other things—the values associated with the quest for *mokṣa;* Śuka, following this overt strand in his father's message, inflicts on his father the suffering inevitably consequent upon any actualization of this quest. In setting this out, our text makes a highly original, even courageous statement, based on a refusal to look away from the human price attached to a basic cultural goal.

The vision that emerges places Śuka at the upper limit of a range of phenomena, all concerned with achieving connection between the human sphere and the transcendent (also pervasive) realm of ultimate truth. The epic presents us with several explicit images of such a connection between this world and other, unseen, dimensions of existence—through sacrifice, for example, the fundamental metaphor for the entire series; but also through riddles *(praśna),* playing with dice, and war. In all these cases, the general rule is that one connects with ultimacy by an act of (usually violent) subtraction. One takes away from the coherent surface reality, which blocks more powerful forms of linkage; by opening a space in the texture of this reality, one allows for movement toward and connection with other, more wholly real, domains.[3] Thus the heroes who die in the *Mahābhārata* war achieve, through their deaths, a return to their original, divine identities, which had been fractured through human birth. Always the fabric of reality has to be unraveled, cut, or torn in order for ultimacy to become present in a dynamic and processual form. One might imagine that Śuka, completely committed to renunciation, could outline a different path, one that would stand in opposition to the violent

3. See Shulman (1992a).

sacrificial world. To our surprise, this is not the case. His renunciation, too, entails a form of self-sacrifice, and his success in this pursuit not only fails to disguise, but actually clarifies and intensifies, the aspect of painful subtraction that we encounter in the more explicitly violent members of this series.

In this respect, Śuka's epithet Āraṇeya, and the whole story of his birth, bear eloquent testimony; they also establish an important linkage with another section of the epic, where similar concerns about the presence of ultimacy, and especially the possibility of linguistic access to it, are central. Śuka is born from the fire-sticks, *araṇī*, rubbed or churned *(√math)*, in a simulation of sexual reproduction to produce the latent fire. The *araṇī* belong properly to a ritual-sacrificial context, and this association is certainly strengthened, as Wendy Doniger has noted, by the role given to Śuka's "mother," Ghṛtācī, whose name means "Sacrificial Ladle Full of Clarified Butter."[4] All of this places Śuka, like Śunaḥśepa, in the realm of that type of sacrifice associated with Vedic ritual—although he later gravitates to the second type, that entails offering up part or parts of the self. Ghṛtācī, of course, like Śuka himself, is given to flight and absence; her task is simply to arouse the sage, intent on producing, more or less alone, a brilliant son. For all intents and purposes, Śuka is truly motherless—or rather, he is born from the womb of sacrifical fire, whose inherently destructive nature may partly condition his fate from birth. His flight toward wholeness and release thus carries traces of original trauma, and also, perhaps, the initial loss of the mother. It is striking that at the very end of his short life, at the crucial moment of transition, Śuka encounters another *apsaras* all too akin to Ghṛtācī: this is Urvaśī, who is responsible for the boy's final act of memory and compassion toward his father. Urvási, we should recall, abandoned *her* human lover Purūravas, who was partly compensated for this terrible loss by the gift of the first *araṇī* fire-sticks. In this case, too, fire serves as the ambiguous vehicle of connection between the human and divine spheres, after an earlier, erotic linkage is traumatically severed; both Śuka/Āraṇeya and Purūravas live in the shadow left by the elusive *apsaras*.

But we can go still further in this direction. There is another

4. Doniger (in press).

famous set of firesticks in the epic—those stolen from a Brahmin in the forest and eventually recovered, in the course of a riddle contest, by Yudhiṣṭhira (the final section of Book 3, known accordingly as the *Āraṇeyaparvan*). Elsewhere I have argued at some length that these firesticks suggest the form of fiery connectedness between domains that is enacted linguistically through the riddling, on the boundary between life and death. Language, as the Upaniṣads often tell us, always contains this burning, destructive aspect, even as it reaches toward truth.[5] The story of Śuka deals with this issue on several levels: by articulating the opposition between Vedic speech and silence; by its interest in the problems of literalization and the surface forms of speech, as in Vyāsa's dialogue with Śiva; above all, in its primary focus on the echo and its meaning. Śuka, the "firestick boy," is also a parrot, echoing others' words; having become the world, he echoes his father's despairing cry; his story is the echo that survives his disappearance. Indeed, the entire narrative unfolds at the triple intersection of speech, echo, and silence, whose intricate relations it seeks to explore. We will examine this matter more systematically below.

For now, I sum up what we have learned at the outset: Śuka shows us something of the experience of renunciation at the level of family relations, where the renouncer is essentially perceived as lost. Vyāsa suffers the consequences of conjuring up in his son the vision of release; this is the suffering of a father who loses his child, albeit to the metaphysical absolute to which he, himself, is committed. In this sense, our story belongs to the *aqedah* prototype, although it must also be classed in a distinctive subtype, as we shall see. In terms of the wider Hindu framework, Śuka may be said to enact, in an extreme fashion, the Vedic sacrificial principle: ultimacy is attained by violent subtraction (in this case, of son from father; or of self from ego and body). Renunciation is not, after all, far removed from sacrifice, in both the senses we have defined. Śuka, paradigmatic renouncer, springs from the sacrificial firesticks and imitates their role of embodying a fiery, partly destructive connection, as we can see or hear in the plaintive, posthumous echo which he reserves for his father.

5. Shulman, (in press b); *Bṛhadāraṇyaka Upaniṣad* 3.9.24.

3

There is a deeper ambiguity about this echo. Glossed by the text as a form of compassion on the part of the son, who remembers his father before disappearing into the cosmos, the echo seems also to carry overtones of mockery. Śuka has surpassed his father, who is left with the somewhat cold comfort of an echo and a shadow. Note that this final act of Śuka's is the first indication that he has any concern at all for his father, and that it takes place only *after* he has gone away, literally taken flight from Vyāsa. There is a sense in which here, as elsewhere in Indian myth, the coinage of aggression is compassion.

Let me put this more simply and directly. This is a story about fathers and sons, and about the oddly complementary aggression they display toward one another. At first glance, I admit, such a statement may appear outlandish. We have just seen the way the issue of loss is poignantly emphasized, and we have noted the tone of melancholy mourning that attaches to Śuka's fulfillment of the renouncer's ideal. Still, such a tone need in no way preclude the possibility that our text is also interested in the theme of rivalry and tension between father and son. I want to argue that this theme is, in fact, basic to the narrative, though it is partly masked by the fact that Vyāsa's double-edged gift to his son coincides with the primary soteriological ideal of this tradition.

It comes down to this. To teach a son Yoga, or *Sāṅkhya* philosophy, or the theory of release, turns out to be a profoundly uninnocent affair. (This is not my point, but the internal perspective of the text.) The motherless son, growing up in a world without women, learns from his father that this world is an arena of sorrow, ultimately to be rejected. Of course, one stresses the word "ultimately"—Vyāsa is in no hurry for Śuka to seek release. Indeed, his message has a basic ambiguity about it, as we can see from the important episode involving his other students: *they* choose to return to the world to propagate Vedic learning; they are fond of ritual sacrifice and study. There is no reason to believe that they are any less true to their teacher's path than is Śuka, who takes the opposite track, who believes that study is wearisome and only *mokṣa* matters. Both paths emerge legitimately out of Vyāsa's instruction; what is striking is that the teacher is left alone at the end, after his pupils actualize these two divergent possibilities latent in his ideology. This image of the bereft teacher is itself endowed with a certain saliency and power. The teacher's role, like that of the parent, is inherently oriented toward becoming redundant.

Nevertheless, despite the ambiguity of the teaching, and despite the conventional wisdom that recommends delaying one's engagement with release, the negation implicit in yogic soteriology does work its magic in Śuka's mind. From this early point in the story—from the first moment Vyāsa teaches his young son about Yoga—relations between father and son build consistently toward the moment of final separation and rejection. Vyāsa's particular responsibility in this respect is clearly brought out in other versions of the story: in the Telugu *Mahābhārata,* for example, Vyāsa observes that his young son is "absorbed in play with the sons of other sages in the *āśrama,* and connected to the world, with no thought for the *ātman*"; Vyāsa puts a stop to this childlike behavior by teaching Śuka the *śāstras* of Yoga and *Sāṅkhya* and other words designed "to separate him entirely from the egoism *(ahaṅkāra)* implicit in having a body and from the possessiveness *(mamatā)* derived from having a family."[6] This is a fairly extraordinary lesson to impress upon a child, even so precocious a child as Śuka; one wonders just what it means to discover that one's body is but a prison, or that one's love for a father is little more than an oppressive chain. Or rather: our story is interested in exploring this very problem, indeed in showing us something of what this teaching means on the level of the child's emerging self in relation to his authoritative, no doubt overpowering father.

In short, this is also a story of growth, study, and maturation, in which tensions between father and son play a necessary part. Such tensions are, in fact, the measure of Śuka's commitment to his father's professed goal: he is intent upon the immediate actualization of the teaching, in the most literal manner, and in opposition to his father's belated expressions of desire (that Śuka remain just one more day, and then, no doubt, another and another). Indeed, this theme of literalization is one of the keys to Śuka's develop-

6. *Mahābhāratamu* of Tikkana, 12.6.257.

ment and, as already indicated, a leitmotif of the story in general. We see it earlier, when Śiva grants Vyāsa's initial request for a son equal to the five elements; Śuka will eventually dissolve himself into these elements. The father's wish is painfully literalized, even as the yogic strand of his teaching will be painfully realized. These two developments run parallel: the son's unexpected adherence, in an uncompromising manner, to the renunciatory ideals entails the unexpectedly literal achievement of Śiva's boon. Moreover, it is difficult to avoid the feeling that Vyāsa's wish already contains, *in nuce,* the seeds of harmful interaction with the all-too-human son about to be born. This sage, who is not without his own form of egoism linked with the ascetic path he has chosen, cannot bring himself to want an ordinary, flawed, needy human being for a son; the child he gets, who internalizes his father's fantasy, leads a life that is entirely faithful to this uneasy, partly destructive inheritance. It is both fitting and ironic that Śuka will ultimately leave his father trapped in the vulnerable, rather helpless mode that Vyāsa originally rejects for his future son.

The father's wish must work itself out: he asks for a superhuman son, and is consequently denied the presence of a living, human one. The indirect, unconscious aggression implicit in the fantasy is externalized and reversed against its source. Still, the process is never overtly articulated in speech; the real dynamics of this troubled relation are hidden under the rhetoric of idealism, renunciation, and release. Here, as often, literalization is itself the vehicle for masked aggression. Often it is a clown or jester who adopts this literalizing mode in his actions, which expose the absurdity and superficiality of speech at the level of literal denotation;[7] and we should bear in mind that Śuka, too, is perceived as a kind of clown, a crazy fool of God. He instinctively renders literal any complex verbal message. Thus, to take another example, he hears from Janaka—whose name, incidentally, literally means "father," as if this teaching were meant to reduplicate Vyāsa's—that he must see the world in himself, or within his Self:

sarvabhūteṣu cātmānaṃ sarvabhūtāni cātmani
sampaśyan nopalipyeta jale vāricaro yathā

7. See Shulman (1985), 180–200.

> One who sees his self in all beings, and all beings in his self, remains unstained, like a fish swimming through water. (312.29)

This statement will later be enacted in the course of Śuka's flight, when he turns himself into the world. (Note, too, how Janaka first offers his impatient student a more nuanced and complicated message, which includes the necessity of going through the first three stages of life *before* seeking release; only afterwards is he won over by Śuka's eagerness and single-minded fixation, to the point where he allows for the possibility of almost immediate attainment of the final goal.)

By literalizing the message, and thereby paring away its ambiguities and potential openness, Śuka succeeds in transcending his father's state (and in leaving his father behind). His triumph is graphically attested in the slightly ironic scene with the bathing *apsarases:* here rivalry between father and son takes the characteristic Sanskritic form of a contest over desirelessness rather than desire. The women intuitively know that Śuka constitutes no erotic threat; Vyāsa, who still seems to know the difference between male and female, fails this test and is ashamed. A strikingly inverted form of competition again hides the deeper tensions between these two figures.

In this world of oblique and displaced hostility, Śuka's adoption of his father's ideology, read in the most literal and limited fashion, becomes, in effect, a method of rejection. Śuka departs without even answering his father's final, pathetic request. Vyāsa is thus effectively punished by his son's success; when Śuka melts away into the world, Vyāsa is finally alone with the echoes and shadows. Vyāsa's teaching merges with Śiva's gift, literally understood and fulfilled. By activating the most extreme, and most world-negating attitude within the teaching, this son at once fulfills, transcends, and punishes his father by a literally self-extinguishing form of obedience. To render this punishment even more cruel, Śuka articulates it as a form of tenderness. Vyāsa's initial, constrained intentionality, so evident in the boon he demands, produces its ironically exact externalization. Fathers, and prospective fathers, should watch their words.

We can now give this pattern a name. Let us identify a "gnostic *aqedah*" type, focused on issues of knowledge and study with reference to the impersonal Absolute and the ideal of release. For Śuka is by no means alone in this process of growing up under the stimulus of paternal instruction pregnant with aggression. Naciketas, the hero of the *Kaṭha Upaniṣad,* also finds his teacher—Death—because of an ambiguous act of violence flowing from the father. Similarly, as we saw at the outset of this study, Varuṇa takes away the life breaths of his son, Bhṛgu, in order to propel Bhṛgu through a hallucinatory journey of initiation in the other world.[8] In all these stories, the father's act of violence against his son is intimately connected to the search for ultimacy, as if aggression of this sort, from father to son, provided the basic instrumentality of learning or knowing. Truth emerges in these texts out of the father's uncompromising, indeed murderous, attack on his son, which functions as a form of initiation. We could also reverse this formulation by stating what seems to be an empirical fact evident from the texts, that is, that overt violence proceeding from the father, accompanied by all the natural, conflictual emotions inherent in this situation, is only properly attested within the Indian *aqedah* model in stories of this "gnostic" type.[9]

4

We must, however, be careful not to reduce the story to this dimension, however central it may appear. The issue of father-son competition is itself subsumed by a more subtle level, in which deeper metaphysical notions come into play. Were this merely a story of fathers and sons vying with one another in the disguised idiom of devotion to ultimacy (hence to one another's ultimate good), we could commend the authors for their audacity and insight—but would we be moved as we are, I believe, when the final moment unfolds, when Vyāsa is met by his absent son's echoing call?

Listen again to the echo: the world responds with the vocative syllable *bhoḥ!* to the father's wailing cry. The echo proceeds out of

8. *Jaiminīya Brāhmaṇa* 1.42–44; *Śatapatha Brāhmaṇa* 11.6.1.1–13; see chapter 1 above. We can now locate this story firmly within the subcategory of the "gnostic *aqedah*".

9. We should also note that this same pattern fits the many stories of teacher-pupil violence (e.g., Śukra and Kaca in *Mahābhārata* 1.71–72); see Goldman (1978).

creation itself, from the trees and mountains and streams. It is an unformed, half-articulate cry, very close, it seems, to the stratum of reality that we think of as wholly "natural"; this is sound itself, unfashioned into speech, a pure world-sound from the boundary of language and nonlanguage, of creation and nothingness—the totality into which Śuka has vanished, leaving only this faint sign.[10] Even the Vedic word, matrix of creation, is at least one stage beyond the lost son's primordial echo. Indeed, as we have seen, the Vedic word has a peculiar place in the story: Nārada protests when he finds the ashram silent, devoid of recitation; Vyāsa and Śuka then begin to recite the Veda, but break off in the presence of the wind; finally, Vyāsa, wandering through the mountains at the top of the world, calls to Śuka in an imitation of proper Vedic speech *(śaikṣeṇa, svareṇa)*. What he receives back is the cruder, more primitive vocative, from a level of being that is antecedent even to the first moment of transition from prelinguistic, inchoate wholeness to a world structured and motivated by the sacred word. At this level, there is always a son calling out in response to his suffering father.

What is the true force of this call? We have already defined one of its aspects, the auditory parallelism to the shadow or reflection that Vyāsa is allowed to see. In both cases, echo and shadow, we sense an underlying metaphysics of loss and substitution; as Pascal says, a person's natural condition is "to see enough to know that he has lost it."[11] On this reading, the echo/shadow speaks to the survivor's self-awareness in a world in which ultimacy is always tantalizingly removed. Vyāsa calls, and the trees and mountains, usually speechless, turn his call into a vocative thrown back at him, demanding his self-recognition. Looking for his son, the father meets with a question, a counter-speech *(prativacas)* which is no true answer but rather a primary, more original utterance directed toward the self in relation to the world. Such are the real modes in which ultimacy inheres in our experience.

In this sense, which takes us beyond the mere recognition of loss or the theory of the traumatic origins of speech, the echo actually

10. A. K. Ramanujan reminds me of the parallel with the wordless "boom" in the Marabar caves in Forster's *Passage to India*.

11. Cited in Cavell (1981), p. 52.

surpasses the original cry, even as Śuka, the son, surpasses his father. Here the *first* sound, even before the Vedic *mantras,* is a kind of echo: the world, in effect, becomes the echo of one's own voice, calling out in longing. Similarly, the shadow/reflection is entirely faithful and real: Śuka, the perfected yogi, sees his own self in the Self, as if he were studying his reflection in a mirror (*ādarśe svām iva cchāyām,* 314.30; this Vedāntic simile is actually Vyāsa's own description of his son, before the latter's departure). Echo and reflection both incorporate an absence, a form of division, yet both embody and re-present, in the sense of making present, the source. Real speech, well-formed to rule, clearly belongs to the world, on this side of the divide in being; the indistinct cry of the echo, a single syllable (*ekākṣaraṃ nādam,* 320.24) like the divine and creative syllable *Oṃ,* issues from the other side of this divide, where Śuka has already become all that is. This single syllable, from some point before creation itself, is released into the space opened up by the father's teaching, which the son internalizes and then literally enacts, and by the separation both have subsequently incurred. Since we are dealing with the transition from ultimacy to the formed and embodied cosmos (and back again), this crying out and the answering question might even be said to constitute the world.

Let me restate this, before looking to further comparisons. Our story delineates a boundary between silence and language; although silence is usually identified with ultimacy, here the son's rough answering syllable, hardly a word, achieves a certain supremacy over both silence and *mantra.* The echo actually supersedes both domains. At the same time, its context within the relations of father and son remains strikingly present, bringing with it the tensions we have noted. Indeed, the single syllable that Śuka leaves behind is all too reminiscent of another son's first, terrible cry:

> There was nothing here in the beginning. This was covered with Death, with hunger—for hunger *is* Death. He made a mind for himself, thinking, "Let me have a self". . . . He divided himself into three parts—fire, sun, and wind, that are the three-fold breath of life. . . . He felt desire for a second self. With his mind, he entered into union with Speech (that is, Death united with hunger); the

> seed of that union became the year, for prior to that there was no year. He carried him for a year and brought him forth. No sooner was the child born than he opened his mouth to swallow him, and the child screamed *"bhāṇ"*—and that scream became Speech. He thought: "If I kill him, I will have but little food." With that Speech, with that self, he brought forth all this—the Ṛc, Yajus, and Sāman, the metres and sacrifices, human beings and animals. And everything that he brought forth, he began to devour.[12]

The world is produced from language, which both preexists (apparently in the form of hunger) and reemerges, no doubt on a different existential plane, out of the infant's first cry of horror. Both "hunger" and "speech" are feminine nouns, and this is the limit of the feminine presence in this myth; all the rest takes place between the primeval male, in his destructive wholeness, and the son born to him. The child's first sight is of his father's gaping mouth, about to swallow him; this perception is thus structured into language and into language-derived reality. Again, the primeval syllable is an inarticulate scream, *bhāṇ* rather than Śuka's *bhoḥ,* produced on the border between creation and the death-filled void. Language united with mind gives structure and existence to time (the year), which then frames the moment of birth. As in the South Indian stories of the Little Devotee, the godhead (identified as Death) is caught up in some form of oral craving—not, this time, for sensual experience as such, directly symbolized by food in the form of the sacrificed child, but rather for an inner fullness that has externalized itself as a dangerously autonomous being, an "other" accessible only through the alternative oral mode of traumatic speech. For our purposes, the essential point is the linkage established here, as in the Śuka story, between language in its root and origins and the tortured binding of father to son: like Śuka, this son is also born from the father alone, and suffers his attack; speech derives from this initial relation, which reproduces itself infinitely in the father's continuous, devouring hunger for his creatures; the son is the father's second self, and as such, together with speech, he serves as the instrument of further

12. *Śatapatha Brāhmaṇa* 10.6.1–5.

creation, hence of further violence. It is as if the world, in the end, were simply this: a hungry father, an anxious son, and the broken syllable that connects them.

Both this text and the story of Śuka concern themselves with the cosmogonic power of speech, and in this they form part of an evolving tradition of speculation that later flowered into various well-known literary expressions. It is by no means unusual to hear in Hindu texts that the cosmos is, in essence, composed of language (more correctly, perhaps, of utterance); or that sound *(śabda)* is the earliest, and primary, medium of creation; or that the first, creative syllable (and therefore language itself) embodies the Absolute *(śabdabrahman)*.[13] In general, such views tend to hold language within a more or less monistic and hierarchical metaphysical frame; thus the earlier, more subtle forms of speech are also, by definition, purer and more encompassing, and very close to ultimate being. But the story of Śuka suggests an alternative, perhaps earlier vision of language as, at base, a choked and shattered cry, a wordless call to the father from a wounded son who has gone away. *This* is the form in which speech generates the world. At its core lies the tangled skein of displaced aggression, oblique utterance, and inevitable separation, in which father and son are bound to one another, and each to the other's truth. Speech proceeding from this core can only be an echo, an open apostrophe, a shadow hidden within words.

As we read the story of Śuka, we naturally think of Narcissus and Echo, with its similar "conjunction of auditory and visual echoes":[14]

Narcissus was born to the nymph Liriope, whom the river-god Cephisus raped. The blind seer Tiresias prophesied that Narcissus would live to old age only if he did not know himself. By the time he turned sixteen, this beautiful boy was loved and sought after by many men and many girls, but, in his pride, he responded to none of them. Among those who loved him was the talkative nymph Echo, who used to distract Juno with her words while Jupiter was making love to other women. As a result, Juno had cursed her to have only the most limited use of her tongue, and, indeed, Echo

13. Thus Bhartṛhari in the *Vākyapadīya;* see Biardeau (1964).
14. Doniger (in press).

could only repeat the end of another's utterance. She followed Narcissus in the forest. "Is there someone here?" called the boy, and she answered, "Here." "Why do you flee from me?" he asked, and heard this same question in reply. "Let us meet," cried Narcissus, and Echo joyfully repeated these words as she came to embrace him. But at this he was startled and drew back, saying, "Don't touch me! I would die before I would give myself to you." Answered Echo, "I would give myself to you."

Shamed, she hid in lonely caves, hiding her face with leaves. Her body withered away out of love, until only her bones and her voice were left; her bones turned to rock, but her voice survives in the woods, where all can hear it. It alone lives on in her.

As he had toyed with Echo, so Narcissus treated others, until one day a rejected lover cursed him to love in just this way, and to fail to attain his beloved. Narcissus came upon a pond of silver, limpid water in the woods, and there he saw his image reflected and fell in love, desiring himself unwittingly, at once burning and igniting. Again and again he tried to kiss the water, to embrace the elusive shadow. In pain he cried out to the forest, "Has anyone loved like me? I delight in what I see, but I cannot find that which I see and love. We are kept apart only by this thin line of water. He too wants to be embraced, for when I stretch out my arms toward him, he reaches out toward me. He smiles as I smile, weeps when I weep. I am he! I feel this, my image does not deceive me. I burn with love for myself. Am I to woo or be wooed? Since what I long for is with me, my very riches have made me poor. It is strange for a lover to wish this, but I want my love to be separate from me." He wept, and the tears, falling into the water, disturbed the image. Now Narcissus became frenzied, calling on his beloved not to disappear. In agony, he tore off his cloak and beat his breast with his hands. His skin turned purple, like a ripening grape, as he bruised and pounded himself, wearing away his body and his strength. Dying, he cried "Alas!," and Echo answered back, "Alas!" "O vainly loved," he wept, "farewell," and Echo responded, "Farewell."

When he arrived in the underworld, he was still staring at his reflection in the waters of the Styx. The Naiads and Dryads mourned him, and Echo carried their cries of grief. As they were preparing the funeral pyre, they discovered that the body was gone, and in its place there was a flower, its yellow heart surrounded by white petals.[15]

Like Śuka, though in a less literal mode, Narcissus takes himself to be the world. His story, too, is about knowledge, specifically self-knowledge in relation to growth and maturation. Narcissus will live only so long as he does not know himself. But what is the nature of the lethal self-knowledge that he acquires? Is it the surface experience of the reflection, that induces love for his perfect body? Or is it rather the awareness of his own fatal self-absorption, as his long soliloquy seems to suggest, with its telling transition from the initial statements of desire for his beloved to the sudden announcement of identity—"I am he!"? In either case, Narcissus reveals an unhappy failure to achieve wholeness, as seen above all in his inability to internalize, indeed even fully to recognize, any external other. He can only toy seductively with others, who are helplessly drawn to his self-sufficiency, while in himself he experiences what Wendy Doniger calls "the devastating reflexivity of perverse erotic love."[16] It is thus fitting that his counterpart should be the linguistically crippled Echo, another stunted self—although Echo, at least, seems tragically capable of a love she cannot voice. Her echoing cry, like Vyāsa's call (and the world's answer), then becomes a mournful iteration of loneliness, a sorrowing, perhaps also reproachful farewell. And, again like Vyāsa, she survives her beloved, although without her body.

In this lies, as well, the essential difference between the two stories: in the Latin myth, Echo, like the mesmerizing reflection in the pool, can only be a derivative and secondary image, bodiless, lacking a life of her own; but Śuka's echo, as we saw, actually transcends its source insofar as it proceeds from the very edge of existence, the point where the Absolute turns into the world. In the Sanskrit text, neither the echo nor the shadow is simply a dead derivative of the lost other, although both are, in some sense, dependent on an absent original. Similarly, Śuka's Self-absorption, unlike Narcissus's, is a form of ultimate self-realization: the one who sees all in his self and his self in all beings has not failed to

15. Paraphrased from Ovid, *Metamorphoses* 3.339–510.
16. Doniger (in press).

mature into personhood, but rather reintegrates his own life into the fragmented cosmos. Narcissus, who loves only himself, whose self is wholly incomplete, can only be loved by an echo. He is, as he tells us, desperate to achieve some kind of separation from his own adored image, however strange this desire might seem in a lover. In the end, he can only lose himself to himself by dying, the supreme instance of separation recognized in his world (although even in Hades he remains fixated on his own image in the Styx!). Śuka, by way of contrast, escapes death by renouncing self-love; his attack on the self is aimed at an identification with the divine Self that permeates *his* world.[17] The striking point is that this ideal form of self-transcendence, like the echo that signals its successful completion, is here seen as burdened by its own poignant residues of pain.

17. Similarly, the Vedānta knows the ideal of the "ego-less personality," who has realized maturity in the freedom of his own divinity: see Murti (1983), 349.

6
Conclusion

'ayin be-mar bochah ve-lev sameach.

The eye weeps bitterly, and the heart is glad.
—Yehuda Ibn-ʿAbbas (Carmi 1981)

1

The Temple in Jerusalem is said to have been built at the site of the *aqedah*. More precisely, tradition tells us that the temple was situated precisely over the thicket where Abraham found the ram, surrogate-victim for his son.[1] The ram, which had been waiting for this moment from the time of creation,[2] was entangled in the thicket by his horns, just as those who listen to this story may find themselves trapped in another hidden, thorny spot. Only such a spot, it seems, properly defines a holy space.

For centuries this story has exercised and tormented readers of the Biblical text. Like the Little Devotee, Abraham stands near the center of his tradition, which treats his act as a supreme, yet also problematic, statement of its values. The story is at once a fundamental paradigm and a complex encapsulation of conflicting themes. For all their singularity and the specificity of the intuitions which produced them, these themes sometimes intersect with those of the Hindu texts we have been studying. I cannot explore the *aqedah* traditions here at any length, partly for fear of becoming entangled in that other thicket; our concern is still to under-

1. Mezudat David ad Psalms 132:6, *meza'nuha besdai yaʿar.*

2. Avot 5:9. Thus the end of the story, i.e., Isaac's physical survival of the trial, preexists its unfolding.

stand the essential themes of the Hindu tales we have been exploring, and the further one takes this exploration, the more incommensurable each of the stories appears in relation to other, perhaps formally similar narratives. It is the distinctive expressive power of each story, even each version, that, in the end, should matter most. Nevertheless, this distinctiveness sometimes emerges more starkly out of contrast: so, before we try to sum up the Indian materials, let us take note of several aspects of the Biblical and Midrashic treatment of this story-type, seen primarily in a comparative vein.

First, as we have noted in relation to the Little Devotee, the Hebrew *aqedah* is a tale of trial and testing *(nisayon),* as the first words of Genesis 22 make clear. We have to try to understand this trial; recall that the Siriyāla myth resorts to this notion only in the later, Telugu versions. What is the meaning and nature of the test? Whose need does it fulfill? In the Talmud,[3] the context is another debate between God and Satan, as in the frame story of Job: Satan sardonically tells God that Abraham, who has made splendid feasts for others, has never offered even a single turtledove to God! God answers him: "He has done nothing that was not for his son—and if I were to say to him, 'Sacrifice your son to me,' he would immediately obey." Hence the need for the trial: God needs proof[4] against the unsettling voice of Satan, the subjunctive voice of doubt. This will be the basic mode of the *aqedah,* one of negative potentiality to be disproved by externalized action. "If *(ilu)* I were to say to him . . ."—everything proceeds from this corrosive "if," where fantasy and fear break into language and thought.

Whose voice does Satan represent in this text? In the *Midrash Rabbah,* the doubt is in Abraham's mind. The Biblical text begins with the phrase, "after these things." What things? The Midrash answers: "the thoughts *(hirhurim)* that were there—Abraham's thoughts. Abraham said to himself: 'I have rejoiced and given joy to others, but I have never put aside for God a single bull or a single ram.' "[5] Another opinion quoted immediately after this pas-

3. Sanhedrin 89b.

4. *pitchon peh* (Rashi on Genesis 22:12): after the trial, God has an answer for those who cannot understand the special love he has for Abraham.

5. *Midrash Rabbah,* Bereshit 55:4.

sage suggests that this same doubt was articulated by the angels, God's heavenly court of law. The uncertainty is apparently widespread enough to emerge in various arenas. Still, it is important to remember that it is God who demands the trial; Satan, as often, gives voice to an inner doubt within the consciousness of his interlocutor. In this culminating drama of Abraham's life, the true end to his spiritual and emotional growth, God is driven to find an answer, in the world of action, to his own skepticism and disquiet. The divine "if" has to be resolved, in a sense, at Abraham's expense, and that of his wife and son.[6]

A strong undercurrent of interpretative comment takes up this theme in the Midrashic sources. God is compared to a teacher who violates the very tenets he seeks to impart to his pupils: "do not seek vengeance or bear a grudge," he says, yet he himself is a vengeful and angry God (Nahum 1:2); "do not put God to a trial," he says in Deuteronomy 6:16—yet he puts Abraham to the test.[7] Indeed, so strong is this need that the *aqedah* is but a reenactment of earlier trials, nine of them, according to the Midrash. Rabbi Hanin offers a bitter comment on this series: After it is all over, the divine voice says with satisfaction, "because you have done this thing (I will bless you)" [Genesis 22:16]. "How can He say this, 'because you have done this thing?' This was the tenth trial—and there was still some doubt?!"[8] That is why the story ends with God's oath to Abraham; for, having gone through this horrific test, Abraham can now demand, 'Swear to me that you will never test me or my son Isaac again.'[9] . . . He knows all too well the propensities of the deity he loves. As the Midrash says in this same passage: "It is like a king who was married to a woman who bore him a son, but he divorced her; he later remarried her, and she bore him a second son, and again he divorced her; and so it went, divorce after divorce, until, after the birth of the tenth son, the children gathered together and demanded of their father that he

6. We cannot expand upon this theme of the traumatic aftereffects of the *aqedah;* suffice it to say that the tradition sometimes connects Isaac's blindness with his experience on the mountain, and Sarah's death with *her* discovery of what almost happened.

7. *Midrash Rabbah,* Bereshit 55:3.

8. Ibid., 56:11.

9. Ibid.

swear never to divorce their mother again." Note that this initiative comes from the children, ostensibly the weaker side of the father-son relation; they take the responsibility for healing their father's destructive needs.

The *aqedah* is, then, first of all, a trial, in which an ambiguity, a negativity, and an uncertain potentiality are to be worked out; and these forces seem, in the eyes of the commentators, to be active within God no less than, and perhaps much more than, in any of the other participants in the story. God's need, focused pathetically in the words of the angel who intervenes to stop the killing, is to know, in some fuller and more convincing way than proleptic fantasy can provide: *ki atah yada'ti,* "for now I know" (that you fear God, 22:12). If the Tamil Śiva is driven toward externalized, sensual experience as the medium of a love defined as truth, the Biblical/Midrashic deity is hungry for knowledge that can be gained only out of the inner torment of his beloved. The doubt that requires testing—that may also constitute, in its own way, the very ground of the love-relationship between these two passionate figures—is properly divine.

It is also striking that this doubt is contextualized by Abraham's history of giving feasts: he has not set aside a single bull or ram, has fed others but never God. The theme of oral incorporation, so central to the South Indian story, enters the *aqedah* materials obliquely in this linkage established by the rabbis. Once there, it resonates strongly with the specific dynamics of a trial, where God demands a victim that he could literally consume. Isaac is bound to an altar situated, like all altars, at the very edge of the living world, at a point of potential transition to reabsorption by the deity. It is in this light, too, that he becomes fully paradigmatic: the knife Abraham carries is called *ma'achelet,* from the root *achol,* "to eat"; "everything that Israel eats in this world is by virtue of that knife."[10]

And yet the sacrifice is averted. Whatever else one can say about the Hebrew *aqedah,* this primary element remains. It is true that, as Spiegel has shown in his beautiful study,[11] there is a strong argument within the tradition to the effect that Isaac was actually

10. Ibid 56:3.
11. Spiegel (1967).

sacrificed. The critical verse 22:19—"and Abraham returned to his boys"—is couched in the singular, the implication being, say the commentators, that Isaac did not come back with his father from the scene of sacrifice. He was, it is said, in Paradise, being healed from the trauma he had undergone. Abraham was allowed after all to shed a quarter of Isaac's blood—enough, that is, to kill him.[12] Once there, on the mountain, neither father nor son could bear to see their commitment to this deed undone; they longed for the knife, for, at the very least, a scar on Isaac's throat.[13] And for the medieval poets, this truth, the necessary reality of the son's sacrifice, furnishes meaning to a paradigm tragically enacted in history.[14] Nevertheless, the Biblical text tells a story of symbolic substitution, which the Midrash also elaborates: as Abraham offered each successive part of the ram, he said, "May this be the equivalent of that part of my son."[15] The subjunctive doubt that gives birth to the trial in the first place—God's articulation of the terrible "if," *ilu*—is resolved through the symbolic subjunctivity of substitution: the ram is killed "as if" it were the boy *(ke'ilu beni shachut, ke'ilue damo zaruq)*.[16] The intended victim is replaced, the trial limited to a rigorous demonstration of intention: it is enough, it seems, for God that father and son are brought to the penultimate point. Unlike the Tamil story, the Biblical *aqedah* does not require the final crossing. Abraham assuages compelling doubt simply by being true.

Modern apologetics to the contrary notwithstanding, this does not seem to be a moral triumph of any kind—a lesson in what *not* to sacrifice. In the Midrash, in fact, it is the still insidious and destructive Satan (Samael) who represents the qualms arising in Abraham's mind—and perhaps the voice of conventional morality as well—during his long journey to the mountain. "Old man," he says to Abraham, "have you lost your heart? You were given this

12. *Tanhuma,* Vayera 23; *Hadar zekenim* 10b, cited with other sources in Spiegel (1967), 7.

13. See sources quoted ibid.; my thanks to Melila Helner-Eshed for discussion of this theme.

14. Thus in the *piyyuṭ* cited by Spiegel. In modern Hebrew poetry, too, the *aqedah* derives its centrality and psychological power from the rooted perception of an ever real and ever repeated sacrifice.

15. *Midrash Rabbah,* Bereshit, 56:9; see Rashi on Genesis 22:13.

16. Ibid.

son when you were one hundred years old—and now you are going to slaughter him?" Abraham answers with enigmatic words of ultimate resignation: *al menat ken,* "indeed so, and for this very reason." Satan then tries his luck with Isaac—just as Śiva seeks to dissuade the intended victim in Śrīnātha's version of the Little Devotee—and meets with the same response. Still, some doubt lingers in the boy's mind, and he turns to Abraham with his question: "Here are the fire and the logs, but where is the sheep to be sacrificed?" (22:7). "God will see to the sheep for the sacrifice, my son." Is this a statement of quiet faith? The Midrash splits it painfully into two: "God will see to the sheep—and, if not, for the sacrifice [will be] my son."[17] And they go off together, one to kill, the other to be killed, both equally ready and united in this truth. There can be no stronger statement of the inherent ambiguity of this moment than this split reading of Abraham's reply: language itself offers no certainty; Abraham cannot know, to the end, what God is actually demanding from him, or why. This is the Kierkegaardian point, anticipated by many centuries in the Midrashic exegesis.

On this reading—admittedly following only one strand of the tradition—the issue of substitution raised above takes on a different meaning. It is not really a matter of symbolic commensurability at all, nor of the paradox engendered in consciousness by the act of symbolic equivalence and displacement—as in the Vedic tale of Śunaḥśepa. Rather, the substitute offering seems designed finally to preclude resolution of the fundamental tension rooted in the initial situation of doubt and testing. This act of sacrifice remains, as the Midrash tells us, on the level of "as if" *(keilu);* there is no conclusive answer to the doubting voice, and no irreversible change in awareness, on either the divine or the human level. The original sacrifice is stopped when the angel speaks, assuring Abraham that now God "knows"—and yet this strange alternation in voice and personae, the suggestive switching away from the direct speech of God in the opening verse to the angel's indirect communication at the climactic instant, is also basic to any understanding of the text. Whose voice is the more real? Did Abraham misunder-

17. *Midrash Rabbah,* Bereshit 56:4.

stand the original command? Is only part of God at peace with this aborted trial?[18]

We could go on in this vein, lifting themes from the inexhaustible sources, pointing at resemblances in the Hindu materials we studied. It would be rewarding, for example, to develop this emerging theme of linguistic doubling and displacement, and the remarkable transitions into eloquent silence, that clearly mark the Biblical text.[19] But I will stop with one last comment, directly linked to the problems suggested in the previous paragraph. Perhaps the most salient divergence from the Indian stories lies just here, in the refusal of the Biblical tale to opt for finality or closure on the level of consciousness. True, the *aqedah* has ineluctable consequences for all the participants, mostly traumatic consequences, as we have seen. But the transformation that takes place in Ciṟuttŏṇṭar and his family, and in those who hear his story—the deep change in awareness than can only abrogate their former lives and translate them into some other, entirely divine realm—does not occur in the minds of Abraham and his son. Perhaps the paradox is never intensified to that point of absolute transition, just as the violent deed toward which the story moves is never achieved. More probably, however, there is a conscious perception embedded in this feature of the text. Irreversible transformation is, perhaps, alien to this tradition, which affirms the normative value and reality of an ever-ambiguous world. It is in this sense that the Rabbi of Gur, following after his Midrashic predecessors, stressed the culmination of the *aqedah* in the prosaic verse 19, which concludes the episode: "And Abraham returned to his boys." This, says the Rabbi of Gur, was the true test—whether, after hearing God speak to him directly, after three days of mental and spiritual torment spent journeying toward the mountain, after binding his son and nearly slaying him in the terrifying presence

18. I am again indebted to Aviva Zornberg for suggesting that the alternation in voice may reflect a deliberate failure to resolve the underlying dilemma.

19. We recall again Auerbach's famous essay on Genesis 22, in the opening chapter of his *Mimesis* (1957). The Jewish sources point to the uneasy role of language throughout this episode; both God and Abraham swallow sentences that they could or should have uttered, only to let them surface "innocently" after the trial.

of the deity, this father could, in the end, come down from the mountain and go home.[20]

2

Let us start again with a different set of premises—that God is always hungry, for example, and riddled with desire. That he is exiled in his divine world, hence driven in longing toward this, human one. That his consequent impact upon *our* world inevitably entails violence and destruction, particularly focused on those who are closest to him here. That this violent impacting, in which God's hunger seeks a human victim, offers the only possibility for deep transformation in that victim's self-knowledge. That such transformation generally proceeds through paradox.

If all of this is true, true to a Tamil devotee's imagination of his deity, then the logic of Ciṟuttŏṇṭar's nightmarish ordeal is the logic of paradox. When Śiva comes to earth, there are no straight lines. Our story depends upon strange and recurring forms of displacement. The god needs, it would appear, to share his motivating hunger and desire; he creates the conditions for this sharing by the ultimate demands he makes on Ciṟuttŏṇṭar, who, as a result, will also experience absence and loss. The equation is then magnified and reversed: total loss—the sacrifice of a son—is taken to its farthest limit, where it touches its opposite, total restoration. Losing all, one gains more than all; but the world has changed, and there is no return. The god's desire, displaced downward onto his devotee, fulfills itself through this reversal: Śiva, we notice, never consumes the meal he has demanded. Apparently sated by his experience of love in this destructive mode, he can return, temporarily, to the abstract reaches of his own world.

Desire is aggressive, a movement toward incorporation. In the South Indian story, this works both ways: God wants to swallow his beloved, while the latter actively seeks to force-feed his deity with that which is dearest and hardest to give. This couple is caught up in the process that A. K. Ramanujan has aptly called "mutual cannibalism."[21] It is hard to say who is inside of whom.

20. I wish to thank Mordechai Beck for reporting this saying of the Rabbi of Gur.

21. Ramanujan (1979), 150–52.

More to the point, it is the crossing of this ambiguous border between inner and outer that produces the movement of transformation. As in most Indian tales of sacrifice, this crossing depends on an initial act of negation, a destructive opening toward self-transcendence: hence the son must truly be killed, the loss experienced as real. In this cultural vision, symbolic substitutes would be entirely out of place.

Let me restate these elements of the Tamil text, in a more abstract and summary manner. In theological terms, we are dealing with desire operating in, and upon, God; its results are, first, a sensory and emotional externalization—a movement from the latent, potential, and abstract to the concrete, visible, and limited—and, second, the violence exacted from the human beings with whom the hungry god comes into contact. Both these elements, the sensual and the violent, represent an ontic claim; they frame a level of being that is perceived as ultimately real, and capable of subsuming other levels. In psychological or emotional terms, on the human level, we find a process of transformation that requires the following components, taken in sequence: a descent to "primitive" feeling, undiluted by symbolic mediation of any kind; an inner movement permeated by this feeling, experienced outwardly as violent subtraction and loss; a cognitive paradox (murderous attack upon what is most wanted or loved), informed by sequential contrast (the alternating and mutually enlivening presence of love and aggression, fear and surrender); the concomitant mixing of existential layers, including the exchange of one's own innerness for that of the other, and, on both sides, the incorporation of this otherness into the self. In existential terms, this transformation, once achieved, goes to the roots of consciousness and can no longer be reversed.

Within the narrative and thematic frame just outlined, various subsidiary themes become important, especially in the later evolution of this story in Tamil and Telugu. Issues of controlling the deity, and making him present in a secure manner, through the sacrificial feeding, appear together with a general emphasis on the problem of autonomy versus heteronomy. In the *Basavapurāṇamu,* the human devotee clearly achieves supremacy in this matter over his capricious, perhaps even malicious, deity. At the same time, the notion of testing enters the tradition, ostensibly of the devotee by the god, but in effect, of the latter by the former. In a world where God wishes to put devotion to the test, the worshiper holds a positive advantage; it is in his power to shame his skeptical opponent, to deny his attempts to reduce the meaning of the sacrificial deed, to demand absolute adherence to the metaphysical vision born of his experience. This human advantage in the power struggle between the two parties may translate into radical rejection of the doubting deity: what kind of a god requires these brutal essays in being, which seem to hurt not only the intended, human victim but also, perhaps even more severely, the living god-part embedded within the devotee who is called to sacrifice? Thus Halāyudha, horror-struck by our story, can turn against Śiva, to the point of excluding him from the very community that is oriented toward his worship.

On the other hand, the meaning that emerges from the story can be radically refashioned in a different direction—that of the playful and sensual intimacy, largely devoid of aggressive or destructive features, that Śrīnātha describes in his Brahminized text. Violence is removed from the texture of the experience, which is no longer conflictual and heavy with loss; any apparent loss can be remedied by the healing power of the imagination, and by the redefinition of being as *vilāsa*—an erotic flux among potential selves, which meet in fleeting moments of desire and miraculous knowledge. Transformative paradox, working through raw and painful emotion, becomes the paradoxical re-creation that is play.

The versions we have studied express the distinctive social milieux in which they are situated; still, they remain part of a single thematic continuum. Missing from this continuum is the Biblical stress on persistent inner doubt operating on the evolving personality as it confronts an unfinished world, with the consequent need for continuous testing and self-revelation. Such tests as do take place in the South Indian Śaiva stories tend to rebound against the deity—as when Cuntaramūrtti suspiciously scrapes the gold Śiva has given him on a touchstone (and discovers, of course, that the god has cheated him once again).[22] Not doubt but the inherent fluidity of emotion—including its strong destructive components,

22. *PP* 3281–92, explicating Cuntaramūrtti's *patikam* 25, on Tirumutukuṉṟam.

and its intimate links with play—fascinate the southern hagiographers and theologian-poets.

This is one type of Hindu *aqedah* tale, and, we can now say, one remarkably remote in spirit and concept from the Biblical type. Indeed, so different are the animating themes that we can allow ourselves to wonder if there is any real justification to the Kierkegaardian formulation of the *aqedah* pattern, with which this book began. In both cases, true, God demands the noninstrumental sacrifice of a son. But on one side, we have the urgency of testing, a confusion in voice, a desperate attempt on the part of the father to discover what is being asked of him, to be true; on the other side, a god seeks for himself the truth of human experience, pregnant with violent loss, in order to trigger human self-transcendence. If we now look again at the Sanskrit stories, we find yet another thematic configuration. The two tales of Śunaḥśepa and Śuka, though widely separated in time and context, both focus on issues of generativity and the grounding of metaphysical issues in the family. They delineate the central paradox of parenthood: the fact that generating children ends in the parents' redundancy. The son, who in some sense embodies his father, ultimately replaces him. Out of this matrix issues the aggression which is so prominently displayed by these fathers against their sons.

But this aggression has another aspect, equally crucial to these stories of the type we have called "gnostic." It is the father's role to teach his son the truth—not the technical means of survival, but the final truth that transforms consciousness and thus creates a new person. This is not a simple task; it seems to depend on confrontation and tension, and it creates ambivalence in both partners; what is worse, it embodies a central stage of dying or being killed, as the old, childish self gives way to the newly conscious person. The fathers in these stories assume this responsibility in the name of ultimacy and ultimate knowledge; in effect, they are prepared to kill their sons for this end. Naciketas is sent by his father to Yama; Varuṇa makes Bhṛgu undergo the same form of violent initiation; Vyāsa teaches his son Yoga out of a similar compelling impulse. In each case, a negative movement directed at the child's natural world, and at the natural presupposition of nurturance on the part of the father toward his son, is the essential feature of this process. The world loses its taken-for-granted wholeness; things are, by definition, other than they seem to our eyes; the father who gave life takes on an angry and rejecting mask. The same pattern is expressed in the well-known Hindu motif of losing one's head (as, for example, the god Gaṇeśa does, at the hands of his jealous father, Śiva):[23] the father's task is to give his son a new head by removing the old one, thereby externalizing, however, the father's own experience of violent displacement.

Knowledge gained in this way is redemptive; we can imagine a reconstructed person, newly alive to the miraculous dimensions of experience, aware of the hidden correspondences, freed of egoism and pride, reintegrated by virtue of the crisis he has undergone. But the bond of dependency on the father/teacher has been cut, and both sides feel loss. In killing his son in the interests of imparting knowledge, the father also kills himself as father. And this process repeats itself through the generations: not only generativity, but also teaching, has a lethal side. Moreover, it is hardly surprising that this form of teaching is itself often informed by destructive contents, as we see from Varuṇa's decoding of his son's nightmarish visions of the other world. As in the sacrifice of the son in the South Indian texts, violent subtraction remains the favored mode of connecting with the real.

And in this sense, both major forms of sacrifice converge: both the ritual based on symbolic equivalences and the literal offering up of parts of the self require the elementary experience of negation. With the exception of Śunaḥśepa, all the stories we have seen privilege the latter mode; in the South Indian texts, especially, the symbolic is consistently subverted by the literal, applied to the realm of affective experience on the part of the innately multiple self. The proper arena for transformation—which, to be meaningful, *must* produce change in the externalized domain of deeds and tangible perception—is this inner world of emotion, where fan-

23. Paul Courtright suggests that this story, too, has an initiatory force: Gaṇeśa is effectively taken out of his mother's world and introduced into the male world of his father by an act of violence on the part of the latter, which destroys the child's former consciousness and develops a new awareness in its place. See Courtright (1985), 107–22. Hindu theories of maturation seem often to depend upon just such a violent sequence involving the total transcendence of one's first "head"; thus Bhairava beheads Brahmā in the interests of transforming a more primitive awareness into a deeper, more divine state. See discussion by von Stietencron (1969).

tasy and ambivalence are always at home; in the end, any sacrifice is enacted here. This is a primary tenet of Tamil Śaiva psychology, as we have seen in the frame story of Maṉunītikaṇṭacoḻaṉ as well as in the case of the Little Devotee. But the Sanskrit sources also sometimes move in this direction, away from the domain of symbolic knowledge toward a literalization and externalization of metaphysical experience. Śuka, the hero of our concluding story, shows the transition most clearly: born out of the first, symbolic mode of sacrifice (the *araṇī,* contextualized by Vedic ritual), he chooses the second, wholly literal one as his goal. The real offering he makes is of his own self, in the context of knowledge gained from his father and confirmed by other teachers; in achieving this, simultaneously living out the god's gift to his father at the most literal level, he becomes—even as he loses—the world.

This way or that, God consumes his creatures. Like the fathers who swallow up their sons, truth preys upon us, absorbing us back into its plenitude. Whether we seek it in love and paradox, like the Tamil devotees, or through the deadly processes of knowledge, like the Upaniṣadic initiates, our hunger can never match its hunger, nor can we sate its need. Indeed, our hunger is perhaps, in the end, only a diminished imitation of the unabating appetite of the Absolute, working upon us or through us in the manifold forms of our desire. Consciousness reaches out, past its limitations, to approach this reality of the devouring deity—toward forms of acceptance and identification, won through transformative emotional and/or cognitive striving; or, as with Halāyudha, toward angry protest in the face of the god's terrible demands. All the stories we have studied confront this reality, recognized as fundamental to the cosmology within which human beings grow to awareness, enfolded in a family that lives out, in each generation, the implications of such a vision. In this field of divine forces continuously impinging on our experience, mothers give birth to children; devoted fathers sacrifice their sons.

Bibliography

(Abbreviations used in the text and notes are given in parentheses)

Texts in Sanskrit, Tamil, and Telugu

Aitareya Brāhmaṇa. Bibliotheca Indica. Calcutta, 1895–96.

Basavapurāṇamu of Pālkuriki Somanātha. Edited by Veṭūri Prabhākara Śāstri. Madras, 1926.

Bhāgavatapurāṇa (BP). Bombay, 1905.

Brahmapurāṇa. Gurumandal Series no. 11. Calcutta, 1959.

Brahmāṇḍapurāṇa. Edited by J. L. Shastri. Delhi, 1973.

Cilappatikāram of Iḷaṅkovaṭikaḷ. Edited by U. Ve. Cāminātaiyar. Madras, 1927.

Ciṟuttŏṇṭanāyaṉār carittirak kummi. Madras, 1974.

Ciṟuttŏṇṭapattaṉkatai. Madras, 1975.

Devībhāgavatapurāṇa. Benares: Paṇḍita pustakālaya, n.d.

Haravilāsamu of Śrīnātha. Madras, 1966.

Hitopadeśa of Nārāyaṇa. Edited by Francis Johnson. Hertford, 1864.

Irāmāvatāram of Kampaṉ. Tiruvāṉmiyūr, 1967.

Jaiminīya Brāhmaṇa. Edited by Raghu Vira and Lokesh Chandra. Nagpur, 1931.

Kaliṅkattupparaṇi of Cayaṅkŏṇṭār. With commentary of Pĕ. Palaṉivela Piḷḷai. Madras, 1975.

Kathāsaritsāgara of Somadeva. Delhi, 1977.

Mahābhārata (MBh). Southern Recension. Edited by P. P. S. Sastri. Madras, 1931–33.

Mahābhāratamu of Tikkana. *Śāntiparvan*. Madras, n.d.
Maṇimekalai of Cīttalaic cāttaṉār. Edited by Na. Mu. Veṅkaṭacāmi Nāṭṭār and Auvai. Cu. Tuṟaicāmippiḷḷai. 2d ed. Madras, 1951.
Pĕriya Purāṇam (PP) of Cekkiḻār. Madras, 1970.
Puṟanāṉūṟu. Edited by U. Ve. Cāminātaiyar. 6th ed. Madras, 1963.
Rāmāyaṇa of Vālmīki (Rām.) Edited by K. Chinnaswami Sastrigal and V. H. Subrahmanya Sastri. Madras, 1958.
Ṛgveda (RV). 6 vols. London, 1849–64.
Śatapatha Brāhmaṇa. Edited by Albrecht Weber. Bibliotheca Indica. Calcutta, 1903–10.
Taittirīya Brāhmaṇa. Calcutta, 1959.
Tevāram of Cuntaramūrttināyaṉār. Tarumapuram, 1964.
Tiruttŏṇṭar tiruvantāti of Nampi Āṇṭār Nampi. Tarumapuram, 1963.
Tiruvācakam of Māṇikkavācakar. Māviṭṭapuram, 1954.
Tiruvāymŏḻi of Nammāḻvār. With commentary of Uttamūr Vīrarākavācāryaṉ. Madras, 1975.
Upaniṣads. Aṣṭādaśa upaniṣadaḥ. Poona, 1958.

Other works

Auerbach, E. 1957. *Mimesis: The Representation of Reality in Western Literature*. Translated by William R. Trask. New York.
Beck, Brenda E. F., Peter J. Claus, Praphulladatta Goswami, and Jawaharlal Handoo. 1987. *Folktales of India*. Chicago and London.
Biardeau, Madeleine. 1964. *Théorie de la connaissance et philosophie de la parole dans le brahmanisme classique*. Paris.
Blackburn, Stuart H. 1987. *Singing of Birth and Death: Texts in Performance*. Philadelphia.
Bose, Tara. 1977. *Folk Tales of Gujarat*. Delhi.
Burrow, Thomas, and M. B. Emereau. 1961. *Dravidian Etymological Dictionary (DED)*. Oxford.
Carmi, T., ed. 1981. *The Penguin Book of Hebrew Verse,* 358. Harmondsworth.
Cavell, Stanley. 1981. *The Senses of Walden*. San Francisco.
Cone, Margaret, and Richard F. Gombrich. 1977. *The Perfect Generosity of Prince Vessantara*. Oxford.
Courtright, Paul B. 1985. *Gaṇeśa, Lord of Obstacles, Lord of Beginnings*. New York.
Doniger, Wendy [O'Flaherty]. 1973. *Asceticism and Eroticism in the Mythology of Śiva*. Oxford.
———. 1976. *The Origins of Evil in Hindu Mythology*. Berkeley.

———. 1980. "Inside and Outside the Mouth of God: The Boundary between Myth and Reality." *Daedalus* 109(2): 93–125.
———. 1985. *Tales of Sex and Violence: Folklore, Sacrifice, and Danger in the Jaiminīya Brāhmaṇa.* Chicago and London.
———, ed. and trans. 1988. *Textual Sources for the Study of Hinduism.* Manchester.
———. 1992. "The Deconstruction of Vedic Horselore in Indian Folklore." In *Festschrift Jan Heesterman.*
———. In press. "Echoes of the *Mahābhārata:* Why is a Parrot the Narrator of the *Bhāgavata Purāṇa* and *Devībhāgavata Purāṇa?*" To appear in *Purāṇa Perennis* edited by Wendy Doniger (in press).
Doniger, Wendy, and Brian Smith. 1989. "Sacrifice and Substitution: Ritual Mystification and Ritual Demystification." *Numen* 36:189–224.
Dorai Rangaswamy, M. A. 1959. *The Religion and Philosophy of Tēvāram.* Madras.
Egnor, Margaret Trawick. See Trawick, Margaret.
Falk, Harry. 1986. *Bruderschaft und Würfelspiel: Untersuchungen der Entwicklungsgeschichte des Vedischen Opfers.* Freiburg.
Feldhaus, Anne. 1990. *Rivers and Cosmology in Maharastra.* Manuscript.
Goldman, R. P. 1978. "Fathers, Sons, and Gurus: Oedipal Conflict in the Sanskrit Epics." *Journal of Indian Philosophy* 6: 325–92.
Gombrich, Richard F. See Cone and Gombrich 1977.
Gumilyov, Nikolai. 1989. *Stiḫotvoreniya i poemi,* 357. Moscow.
Handelman, Don. 1992. "Passages to Play: Paradox and Process." *Play and Culture* 5:1–19.
Hardy, Friedhelm. 1983. *Viraha-bhakti: The Early History of Kṛṣṇa Devotion in South India.* Delhi.
Hart, George. 1979. "The Little Devotee: Cēkkiḻār's Story of Ciṟuttoṇṭar." In M. Nagatomi, B. K. Matilal, J. M. Masson, and E. Dimock, eds., *Sanskrit and Indian Studies: Essays in honour of Daniel H. H. Ingalls,* 217–36. Dordrecht, 1979.
Heesterman, Jan. 1957. *The Ancient Indian Royal Consecration: The Rājasūya Described according to the Yajus Texts and Annotated.* The Hague.
———. 1962. "Vrātya and Sacrifice." *Indo-Iranian Journal* 6:1–37.
———. 1964. "Brahmin, Ritual, and Renouncer." *Wiener Zeitschrift für die Kunde Süd- und Ostasiens* 8:1–31.
———. 1967. "The Case of the Severed Head." *Wiener Zeitschrift für die Kunde Süd- und Ostasiens* 11:22–43.
Hudson, D. Dennis. 1989. "Violent and Fanatical Devotion among the

Nāyaṉārs: A Study in the *Periya Purāṇam* of Cēkkiḻār." In Alf Hiltebeitel, ed., *Criminal Gods and Demon Devotees,* 373–404. Albany, 1989.
Johnson, Willard. 1980. *Poetry and Speculation of the Ṛg Veda.* Berkeley.
Kierkegaard, Søren. [1843] 1954. *Fear and Trembling.* Translated by Walter Lowrie. New York.
Malamoud, Charles. 1989. *Cuire le monde: Rite et pensée dans l'inde ancienne.* Paris.
———. See Renou 1978.
Mandelstam, Osip. 1977. *Selected Essays.* Translated by Sidney Monas. Austin and London.
Midrash Rabbah. With commentary by A. A. Halevi. Tel Aviv, 1956.
Mines, Mattison. 1984. *The Warrior Merchants: Textiles, Trade, and Territory in South India.* Cambridge.
Monier-Williams, Monier. 1899. *A Sanskrit-English Dictionary.* Oxford.
Murti, T. V. R. 1983. *Studies in Indian Thought.* Edited by Harold Coward. Delhi.
Nandimath, S. C. 1942. *A Handbook of Virasaivism.* Dharwar.
Narayana Rao, Velcheru. 1986. "Epics and Ideologies: Six Telugu Folk Epics." In S. Blackburn and A. K. Ramanujan, eds., *Another Harmony: New Essays on the Folklore of India,* 131–64. Berkeley, 1986.
———. 1990. *Śiva's Warriors: The Basava Purāṇa of Pālkuriki Somanātha.* Princeton.
Narayana Rao, Velcheru, with A. K. Ramanujan and D. Shulman. In press. *When God Is a Customer: Telugu Courtesan Songs by Kṣetrayya and Others.* Berkeley.
Narayana Rao, Velcheru, with David Shulman and Sanjay Subrahmanyam. 1992. *Symbols of Substance: Court and State in Nāyaka Tamil Nadu.* Delhi.
Obeyesekere, Gananath. 1990. *The Work of Culture: Symbolic Transformation in Psychoanalysis and Anthropology.* Chicago and London.
O'Flaherty, Wendy Doniger. See Doniger, Wendy.
Ovid. *Metamorphoses.* Edited and translated by D. E. Hill. Warminster, Wiltshire, 1985.
Penzer, N. M., ed. 1924–28. *The Ocean of Story.* Translated by C. H. Tawney. 10 vols. London.
Philo of Alexandria. *De Abrahamo.* Edited and translated by F. H. Colson. Loeb Classics Library, 6. Cambridge, Mass., 1935.
Ramanujan, A. K. 1973. *Speaking of Śiva.* Harmondsworth.
———. 1979. *Hymns for the Drowning. Poems for Viṣṇu by Nammāḻvār.* Princeton.
———. 1983. "The Indian Oedipus." In Lowell Edmunds and Alan Dundes, eds., *Oedipus, A Folklore Casebook.* New York and London.

———. 1985. *Poems of Love and War.* New York.
———. 1986. "Two Realms of Kannada Folklore." In S. Blackburn and A. K. Ramanujan, eds., *Another Harmony: New Essays on the Folklore of India,* 41–75. Berkeley.
———. See Narayana Rao, Ramanujan, and Shulman, in press.
Renou, Louis. 1978. *L'Inde fondamentale.* Edited by Charles Malamoud. Paris.
Rilke, Rainer. [1934] 1962. *Letters to a Young Poet,* 50. Translated by M. D. Herter Norton. New York.
Robinson, William Henry. 1911. *The Golden Legend of India, or, the Story of India's God-Given Cynosure (Śunaḥśepa-Devarāta).* London.
Roghair, Gene J. 1982. *The Epic of Palnāḍu: A Study and Translation of Palnāṭi vīrula katha.* Oxford.
Shulman, David. 1983. "Notes on the Kālāntaka Myth at Tirukkaḍavūr." In K. V. Raman et al., eds., *Śrīnidhiḥ: Perspectives in Indian Archaeology, Art, and Culture (Shri K. R. Srinivasan Festschrift),* 267–74. Madras.
———. 1985. *The King and the Clown in South Indian Myth and Poetry.* Princeton.
———. 1986. "Terror of Symbols and Symbols of Terror: Notes on the Myth of Śiva as Sthāṇu." *History of Religions* 26:101–24.
———. 1990. *Songs of the Harsh Devotee: The Tēvāram of Cuntaramūrttināyaṉār.* Philadelphia.
———. 1992a. "Devana and Daiva." *Festschrift Jan Heesterman.* Leiden.
———. 1992b. "Die Dynamik der Sektenbildung im mittelalterlichen Südindien." In S. N. Eisenstadt, ed., *Kulturen der Achsenzeit* 2, 102–28. Frankfurt, 1992.
———. In press a. "Remaking a Purāṇa: The Rescue of Gajendra in Potana's *Mahābhāgavatamu.*" To appear in Purāṇa Perennis, edited by Wendy Doniger (in press).
———. In press b. "The Yakṣa's Questions." To appear in a volume edited by Galit Hasan-Rokem and D. Shulman (in press).
———. See Narayana Rao, Ramanujan, and Shulman, in press.
———. See Narayana Rao, Shulman, and Subrahmanyam 1992.
Simon, Bennet. 1988. *Tragic Drama and the Family: Psychoanalytic Studies from Aeschylus to Beckett.* New Haven and London.
Sivaraman, K. 1973. *Saivism in Philosophical Perspective.* Delhi.
Sontheimer, Günther-Dietz. 1981. "Dasarā at Devaraguḍḍa: Ritual and Play in the Cult of Mailār/Khaṇḍobā." *South Asian Digest of Regional Writing* 10:1–27.
———. 1989. "Between Ghost and God: A Folk Deity of the Deccan." In

Alf Hiltebeitel, ed., *Criminal Gods and Demon Devotees,* 299–338. Albany.

South Indian Inscriptions (SII). Madras. 1890–

Spiegel, Shalom. 1967. *The Last Trial.* New York.

Subrahmanyam, Sanjay. See Narayana Rao, 1992.

Trawick, Margaret [Egnor]. 1978. "The Sacred Spell and Other Conceptions of Life in Tamil Culture." Ph.D. dissertation, University of Chicago.

———. 1980. "On the Meaning of Śakti to Women in Tamil Nadu." In Susan Wadley, ed., *The Powers of Tamil Women,* 1–34. Syracuse.

———. 1990. *Notes on Love in a Tamil Family.* Berkeley.

Vernant, Jean-Pierre. 1982. "From Oedipus to Periander: Lameness, Tyranny, Incest in Legend and History." *Arethusa* 15:19–37.

———. 1988. *Myth and Society in Ancient Greece.* New York.

von Stietencron, Heinrich. 1969. "Bhairava." *Zeitschrift der Deutschen Morgenländischen Gesellschaft.* Supplement 1, Vorträge, Teil 3, pp. 863–71.

Weller, Friedrich. 1956. "Die Legende von Śunaḥśepa im *Aitareya Brāhmana* und *Śāṅkhāyana Śrauta Sūtra.*" Berichte über die Verhandlungen der Sachsischen Akademie der Wissenschaften zu Leipzig, Philologische-historische Klasse (Berlin) 102(2):8–21.

White, David Gordon. 1986. "Śunaḥśepa Unbound." *Revue de l'histoire des religions* 203(3):227–62.

———. 1991. *Myths of the Dog-Man.* Chicago and London.

Index